hotels · haciendas · spas

mexicochic

hotels • haciendas • spas

mexicochic

text foo mei zee • barbara kastelein

BOLDING BOOKS

publisher'sacknowledgments

There are so many people to thank for their contribution to this book.

The wonderful hotels in Mexico showcased here—thanks for the inspiration. Rafael Micha of HABITA and Deseo [Hotel + Lounge] for his excellent suggestions and fabulous hospitality; Jean Franken and colleagues of Starwood Hotels and Resorts who have supported the book from start to finish; the Mexico Tourism Board for its warm welcome, precious contacts and resources, including some of the stunning photographs featured.

Melisa Teo and colleagues at Editions Didier Millet for delivering a quality product; Juan Ignacio Steta of Aeromar, José Luis Arce of Dollar Rent A Car and José Luis Fernádez de la Maza for their enthusiasm for and participation in the project. My thanks to Foo Mei Zee and Barbara Kastelein for juggling maternal and editorial responsibilities.

Above all, I am grateful to Manuel Diaz Cebrian who conceived this project, and offered plenty of valuable insights into Mexico and advice on the book's content. Finally, many thanks to Andrew Thomas for introducing me to Manuel!

I hope you'll discover in *Mexico Chic* the magic of the country, its illustrious history, people, culture, cuisine and countless areas of fascination, as we did in the course of producing this book. Enjoy it all in style and comfort, as we would, from the luxurious hotels recommended in the following pages.

Nigel Bolding

managing editor
melisa teo

assistant editors
lynette quek • ng wei chian

designers
annie teo • yolande lim

production manager
sin kam cheong

first published in 2003 by
bolding books
16th floor royex house
5 aldermanbury square
london EC2V7hr
email: nigel.bolding@theworldsbesthotels.com

designed and produced by
editions didier millet pte ltd
121 telok ayer street, #03-01
singapore 068590
email: edm@edmbooks.com.sg
website: www.edmbooks.com

©2003 bolding books
design and layout © editions didier millet pte ltd

Printed in Singapore

isbn: 981-4155-01-2

COVER CAPTIONS:
1–3: W Mexico City.
4: Church of Santo Domingo in Oaxaca City.
5: Local dresses from Cuetzalan, Puebla.
6: Sunset on the Pacific coast.
7: Uxmal ruins in Yucatán.
8: Mexican cowboy.
9: The Cathedral of Tlaxcala.
10: Desert cactus.
11: The Yellow City, Izamal, in Yucatán.
12: Camino Real Oaxaca.
13–18: Verana hotel in Jalisco.
19: Hacienda Santa Rosa in Yucatán.
20–22: Deseo [Hotel + Lounge] in Quintana Roo.

PAGE 2: *Deseo's sumptuous daybeds with billowing canopies.*

THIS PAGE AND OPPOSITE: *The hip set is flocking to chic hotels such as Deseo [Hotel + Lounge] in the Riviera Maya.*

PAGE 8 AND 9: *Views of the Pacific ocean from Verana.*

contents

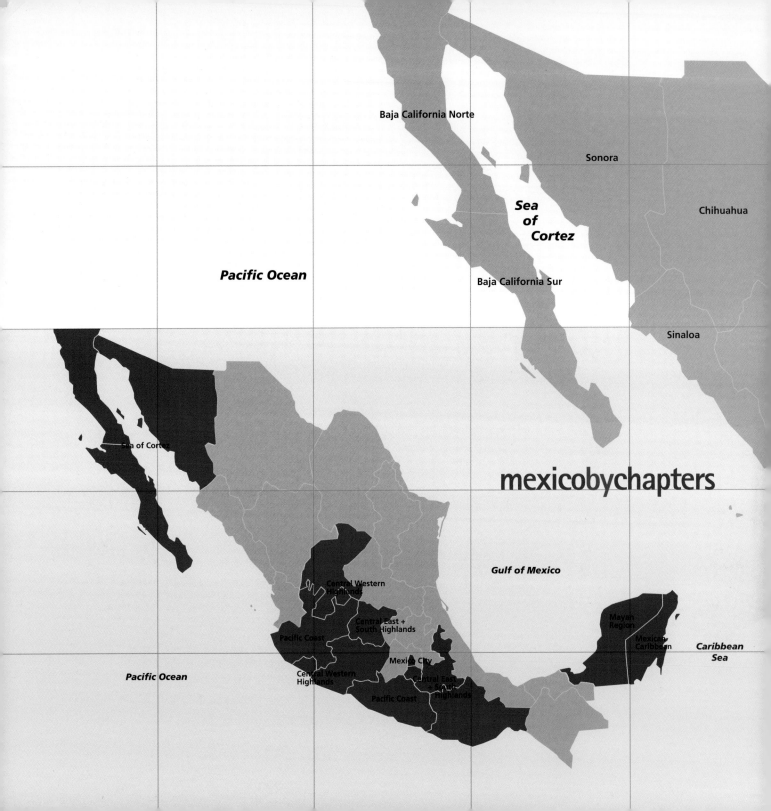

Baja California Norte

Sonora

Chihuahua

Sea
of
Cortez

Pacific Ocean

Baja California Sur

Sinaloa

Sea of Cortez

mexicobychapters

Central Western
Highlands

Gulf of Mexico

Central East +
South Highlands

Mayan
Region

Pacific Coast

Mexican
Caribbean

Caribbean
Sea

Pacific Ocean

Mexico City

Central Western
Highlands

Central East
+ South
Highlands

Pacific Coast

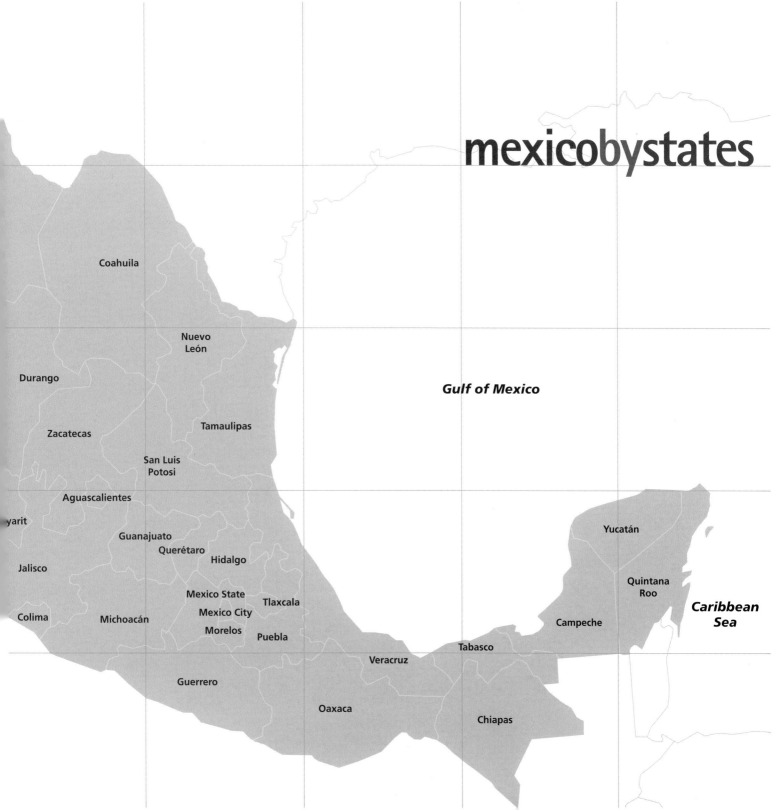

mexicobystates

Coahuila

Nuevo León

Durango

Zacatecas

Tamaulipas

San Luis Potosi

Aguascalientes

yarit

Guanajuato

Querétaro

Hidalgo

Jalisco

Mexico State

Tlaxcala

Colima

Mexico City

Michoacán

Morelos

Puebla

Guerrero

Veracruz

Oaxaca

Tabasco

Chiapas

Yucatán

Quintana Roo

Campeche

Gulf of Mexico

Caribbean Sea

introduction

mexico: land of contrasts

Mexico is an experience worlds apart from anywhere else. Offering infinite opportunities, it lures with its warmth, bright colours, intriguing smells and beguiling music. And yet, it is inaccurate to depict the real nature of Mexico quite so simply, as it encompasses a kaleidoscope of contrasts—of landscapes, architecture, culture, religion—offering much drama and excitement to the visitor.

You'll have to live here—or return many times—to even attempt to comprehend this mammoth expanse of land. It is a deeply seductive country that many find irresistible, with its balmy climate, wide-open spaces, natural beauty and friendly people.

The best advice for first-time visitors: read as much as you can about Mexico's vastly different regions and plan an itinerary which isn't too ambitious.

In this book, you'll find each chapter providing enough activities or attractions for a 10-day vacation or more. There are also suggestions for visitors of Mexico City to include nearby states such as Morelos or Puebla, and historic destinations such as Oaxaca or Morelia. Whatever you do, don't miss the beaches of Acapulco and the Riviera Maya!

fiery food + daring drinks

If you have an adventurous palate or enjoy spicy food, you'll be well rewarded in Mexico, with its many fiery dishes such as camarones a la diabla (spicy prawns) and albóndigas en salsa chipotle (meatballs in smoked chilli sauce). But it isn't just the spices that pervade. Mexican cuisine is considered to be almost as complex as French and Chinese, influenced by the country's 40 different regions.

Icons of Mexican cuisine must surely be the soft and aromatic corn tortillas (made of corn flour), frijoles (beans), chillies and arroz (rice). Corn tortillas, when filled and folded with ingredients like wild mushrooms or cooked zucchini flowers, are called tacos. When they are stuffed with cheese, folded and grilled, they are called quesadillas. Often served in a basket with a meal, tortillas are the equivalent of bread in Mexico.

While tequila is Mexico's national drink, the country's true speciality is jugos or freshly squeezed fruit juices. Take the opportunity to sample native concoctions like

THIS PAGE (FROM TOP): *The use of bold colours such as azul añil (indigo) is traditional for Mexican houses; fruit—fresh and pickled—are savoured in abundance.*
OPPOSITE: *Acapulco twinkling in endless activity at night.*

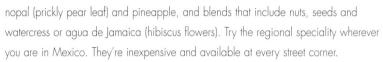

nopal (prickly pear leaf) and pineapple, and blends that include nuts, seeds and watercress or agua de Jamaica (hibiscus flowers). Try the regional speciality wherever you are in Mexico. They're inexpensive and available at every street corner.

A dish that's not so well-known outside of Mexico is sopa seca or 'dry' soup, served between courses, usually during lunch. Sopa seca is technically not a soup, but a dish made from rice, vermicelli, or dry tortilla strips combined with tomatoes, onions and garlic. Sopa de elote, a sweet corn soup, is served at the start of a meal. But when followed by sopa de arroz or sopa de pasta, you can expect little dishes of rice or pasta simmered in tomato or chicken stock, which make excellent appetisers.

Don't restrict your taste of Mexico to traditional restaurants or modern cafés; markets offer an amazing variety of authentic flavours as well. And true connoisseurs never miss touring the local markets where colourful displays of fresh fruit, herbs and flowers fill the air with heady aromas. These markets often offer places to try Mexican cuisine, ranging from small stalls to luncheon counters and cosy restaurants.

Tequila is the infamous spirit of Mexico, usually drunk straight or with a chaser. Some may have heard of its cheaper cousin mescal, a cruder and smokier version of tequila sold with a worm in the bottle. Very few would have heard of pulque, made from the fermented sap of agave plants. Slightly slimy, milky and sour, it is a potent drink that's close to extinction, and worth trying if you find it in Puebla or the few remaining pulquerias in Mexico City.

Beach drinks include the margarita made with tequila and lime juice, and served in a salt-rimmed glass; the cuba libre (rum and coke); and piña colada with its refreshing smoothie-like consistency. Lighter in taste, cheaper and less alcoholic than many European beers, cerveza or Mexican beer is just right for the climate and is often mixed with chasers.

A spicy beer cocktail concocted in true Mexican imbibing tradition is the michelada (my cold beer), which is beer mixed with lime juice (preferably squeezed from Key lime), salt and ice—sometimes with the addition of Maggi seasoning and pepper—served in a long straight glass rimmed with salt. A favourite with Mexicans, there are many versions of this condiment-spiked drink in the country.

THIS PAGE (FROM LEFT):
Traditional Mexican fare
prepared with a delicate touch
following age-old recipes;
cocktails at a Western-
style cantina.

OPPOSITE (FROM TOP): Restaurant
with a priceless view of Morelia;
Mexicans are some of the
world's biggest consumers
of soft drinks.

south, mid or north america?

With its Hispanic culture and exotic surroundings, it's not surprising that some people think Mexico is in South America. Christmas does take place in 'winter' here, although the weather is so good, you can expect to sunbathe all day long in Huatulco and dine outdoors in Guadalajara. The closest you'll ever come to winter in Zihuatanejo or Mérida is sipping on an icy margarita.

Geographically speaking, Mexico is in North America. Mexicans will feel offended if they are referred to as South Americans—not because they have anything against their southern cousins—but because it reveals ignorance of their country's location and heritage.

It's easy to mistake Mexico as Central America, alongside countries like Guatemala and Honduras, with which it shares a few linguistic, culinary and cultural features. But this is incorrect too. While the term Mesoamerica (Middle America) includes the southern part of Mexico and parts of the Central American region, mislabelling Mexico as Central America is also offensive for a confluence of reasons.

Past instability and US military presence in parts of Central America have thrown into question the autonomous nationhood of some of those countries. This, along with the region's poverty, are elements Mexico does not wish to be associated with. The term that works for Mexico is Latin America, which refers to its colonisation by the Spanish.

An important geographical feature that marks Mexico's landscape is the poetically-named 'Ring of Fire', a volcanic zone that extends south to Nicaragua. The volcanoes, most of them dormant, are breathtakingly beautiful. The highest snow-capped peak at 18,400 ft (5,608 m) is Citlaltépetl (Star Mountain), also known as Pico de Orizaba, which lies between Mexico and the gulf coast. Then follows Popocatépetl (Smoking Mountain) at 17,887 ft (5,452 m) and Iztaccíhuatl (White Woman). Visitors can climb Citlaltépetl and Iztaccíhuatl with the help of a guide.

Tropical storms appear on the coast in the rainy season (from June to October) but are usually short-lived. For practical purposes it is advisable to check the climate in the areas where you are going to in advance, including the average temperatures for the time of year, so you can pack accordingly.

people + pyramids

Mexico has a population of over 100 million people, 20 million of whom live in Mexico City and the metropolitan area. The vast majority of Mexicans are mestizo—people of mixed ancestry such as Spanish and Indian, while Catholicism is the dominant religion.

Before the Spanish conquest in 1521, Mexico had seen a series of different ancient civilisations: the Maya in the southeast, the Olmecs on the gulf coast, the Zapotecs in Oaxaca and also in the southeast; the Tarascans or Purépecha in Michoacán, and the Totonacs from Veracruz in the east. The Aztecs, who were fierce warriors with bloodthirsty traditions, were the predominant and most powerful group when Hernán Cortés arrived.

Originally a nomadic tribe, they had settled in Mexico for about 200 years until the Spanish arrived and destroyed their empire. The Aztec ruler was King Moctezuma II and the capital was the Great Tenochtitlán, built on the same site where Mexico City now stands.

Mexico's famous pyramids and ceremonial sites were painstakingly built without metal tools by these ancient civilisations. The term 'pre-Hispanic' is commonly used in Mexico to refer to the periods of history, culture, architecture, craft, language and even cuisine, before the Spanish conquest.

Descendants of these groups live on, although less than 10 per cent of Mexicans are full-blooded Indians, many who live in considerable poverty and rural isolation. Migration to urban centres and pervasive racism in Mexican culture has led many people of Indian backgrounds to drop their indigenous language and roots. However, traditions in dance, music and other customs do continue to be practiced during special occasions.

Doing your own research before you traverse these highly elaborate pyramids will help you piece together their history for a more interesting and rewarding visit.

Independence was finally gained under the leadership of royalist general Agustín de Iturbide in 1821.

yesterday's conquistadors, today's politicians

Once the Spanish conquered Mexico, the colony was named Nueva España (New Spain). The remaining indigenous people who survived the battles and European diseases became slaves. They either worked on the land granted by the Spanish to Cortés' soldiers or had to pay tributes to the crown. By the 17th century, their numbers had declined dramatically. Higher up the socio-economic ladder were the mestizos, who were then followed by the criollos—people of Spanish parentage born in the New World. The colonists who were born in Spain—nicknamed 'peninsulares' or 'gachupines'—were aristocracy, and wielded political power however humble their origins. At the bottom of the rung were the indigenous people and African slaves.

The movement for independence from Spain crystallised in 1810, under the leadership of a charismatic criollo priest called Miguel Hidalgo. On September 16, he uttered his famous cry to rebellion, now known as 'El Grito (shout)' and led troops from the town of Dolores in Hidalgo towards Mexico City. They were defeated, and he was executed the following year. José María Morelos, another priest, took up the torch but was killed in 1815. Independence was finally gained under the leadership of royalist general Agustín de Iturbide in 1821.

Mexico's revolution in 1910 was a complicated affair that followed 33 years of dictatorship under Porfirio Díaz, a period known as the Porfiriato. A decade of civil war followed, and relative stability began in the 1920s.

In 2000, pressures for a more convincing democracy broke 70 years of party rule by the Partido Revolucionario Institucional (P.R.I. or Institutional Revolutionary Party). Vicente Fox of the right-of-centre Partido de Accíon Nacional (P.A.N. or National Action Party) took the helm for six years as Mexico's first non-P.R.I. president in over half a century.

Although Fox's popularity dipped after failing to deliver many of his electoral promises, he has brought a degree of transparency and accountability to Mexican politics that was previously unheard of. The third major party is the left wing Democratic Revolution Party (P.R.D.) which has a high profile in the capital, led by the outspoken mayor of Mexico City, Andrés Manuel López Obrador.

THIS PAGE (FROM TOP): Independence Day celebrations; once a string of giant lakes, Mexico City now abounds with symbolic monuments like the Angel of Independence.

OPPOSITE: The city's zócalo is marked with a giant flag, the symbol of national pride and celebration.

fiestas

The most widely celebrated public holidays in Mexico are Independence Day on September 16, and Cinco de Mayo on May 5, which is the celebration of the Battle of Puebla (when Mexico defeated French invaders in Puebla state in 1862).

Independence Day is marked with a flurry of flags lining the streets and official buildings throughout the month of September. And in Puebla, when the festivities take place in May, bullfights are staged regularly, museums and restaurants hold special events, and fairs emerge all over the state. Expect to enjoy street performances, open-air concerts, cockfights, bullfights and sporting events.

The most important religious holiday is Semana Santa (Holy Week) held in March or April. Also associated with Easter is Carnival, held on the week before Lent (usually in February or March). Veracruz's sizzling nine-day Carnival celebrations on the gulf coast are reputed to be the largest after Rio de Janeiro in Brazil, and are truly exuberant—colourful parades snake through the city's streets daily while fireworks, dance performances, salsa music and handicraft shows add much vibrance. From the mountainous villages in Oaxaca to the dusty towns of Puebla, each town has its own special way of celebrating Carnival.

One of Mexico's most intriguing religious festivals is Día de Muertos or Day of the Dead, which begins on the eve of All Souls' Day on November 1. The indigenous people believe that the souls of the dead return each year to commune with their living relatives. In the villages around Lake Pátzcuaro, they blend solemnity with festivities in an all-night vigil to remember and honour their deceased relatives.

Another festival unique to the country is that of Our Lady of Guadalupe on December 12. As Mexico's patron saint, she remains a symbol of tremendous political, religious and cultural power, and the Basílica de Guadalupe in the north of Mexico City is where millions of pilgrims head every year.

It is often joked that Mexico is permanently on holiday as there is always a fiesta going on. You may find yourself being woken one morning to the sound of firecrackers, or to the tunes of Las Mañanitas, one of Mexico's traditional celebratory songs.

THIS PAGE: *Sombre processions are held throughout Mexico during Semana Santa.*

OPPOSITE: *The charro (Mexican cowboy) is still prized for his horsemanship at rodeos.*

It is often joked that Mexico is permanently on holiday as there is always a fiesta going on.

mexicancaribbean

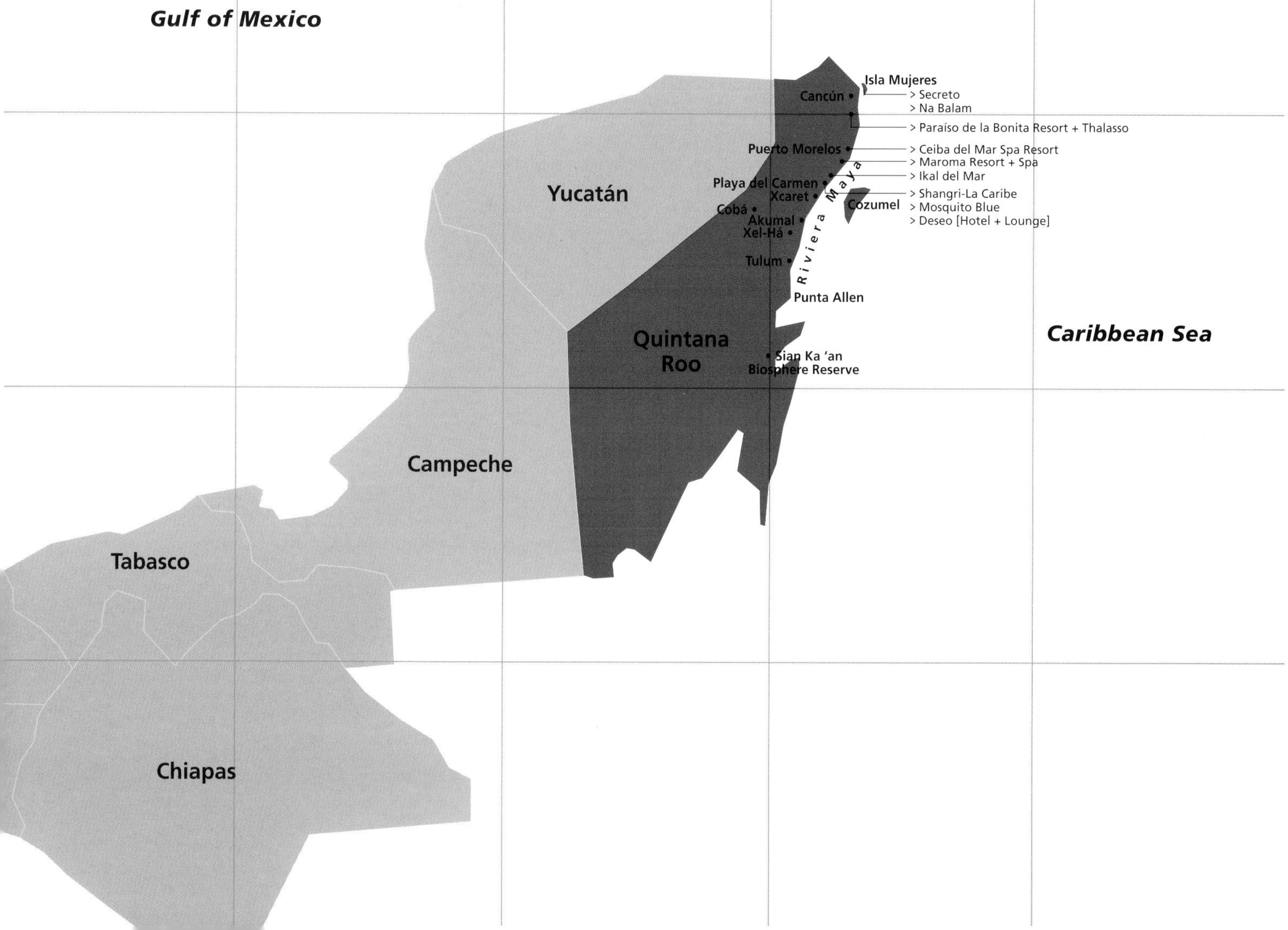

Gulf of Mexico

Isla Mujeres

Cancún
> Secreto
> Na Balam

> Paraíso de la Bonita Resort + Thalasso

Puerto Morelos
> Ceiba del Mar Spa Resort
> Maroma Resort + Spa
> Ikal del Mar

Playa del Carmen
Xcaret
Cobá
Akumal
Xel-Há

Cozumel
> Shangri-La Caribe
> Mosquito Blue
> Deseo [Hotel + Lounge]

Yucatán

Riviera Maya

Tulum

Punta Allen

Caribbean Sea

Quintana Roo

Sian Ka 'an
Biosphere Reserve

Campeche

Tabasco

Chiapas

blue lagoon

Quintana Roo (pronounced as 'kin-tana-row'), the youngest state in Mexico, is where you find all 534 miles (860 km) of the country's Caribbean coastline. In this endless stretch of sea, luminous shades of blue—from sapphire, cobalt and beryl to azure and turquoise—undulate in the light, creating a visual feast. For many visitors, the soft white sands, crystalline waters and unspoiled beauty of Quintana Roo easily match their definition of paradise.

Located on the eastern side of the Yucatán Peninsula, sharing its southern border with Belize, this state faces the Great Mayan Reef, the second-largest coral reef in the world after the Great Barrier Reef of Australia. It is a treasure trove of great biological diversity, teeming with kaleidoscopic coral formations and providing a refuge for tropical fish, sea turtles, dolphins and sea horses. Inland, there are colourful flashes of bird life, the odd jaguar and puma, as well as exotic creatures ranging from the tapir and anteater to the howler monkey.

Another natural wonder of this region is the cenote or sinkhole. The Peninsula is largely a low, flat tableland of porous limestone. Light rainfall is absorbed by the rocks so there are no rivers or lakes above ground. Instead, Quintana Roo and its neighbouring Yucatán state have many underground rivers, lakes and caves with stalactite and stalagmite formations, and incredibly blue waters with striking visibility. There are various types of cenotes—some completely underground or semi-underground—others at land level like ponds or open wells. Many are accessible for swimming and cave-diving, but you should always go with a guide armed with appropriate equipment.

The state is also known for its ecological parks and tropical reserves, with over a quarter of its territory or 31,594 sq miles (50,843 sq km), being protected land. The Sian Ka'an (Where the Sky Begins) Biosphere Reserve is a UNESCO World Heritage Site occupying over 2,383 sq miles (6,172 sq km) of land—amounting to 10 per cent of the state—and more than 62 miles (100 km) of coral reef. With only about 1,000 local residents, mostly Maya, this is one of the last undeveloped

PAGE 22: The breathtaking colour and sensuality of a Caribbean beach provide soothing respite.

THIS PAGE: Gentle surf and beautiful reefs make for excellent snorkelling in the waters of Playa del Carmen.

OPPOSITE: Palapa roofs offer shade from soaring temperatures.

Another natural wonder of this region is the cenote or sinkhole.

stretches of coastline in Latin America, spilling over with mangrove swamps, small islands, watery cays, savannas and tropical forests.

Over 20 unexcavated ruins lie here, linked by a canal system. An extensive chain of freshwater and coastal lagoons provides a haven for fishing, and only selected lodges are permitted to promote the sport. A map is available at the entrance, but to see the sites you are advised to take a guided boat tour offered by the non-profit organisation, Los Amigos de Sian Ka'an (The Friends of Sian Ka'an).

Further north, ecological parks such as Xel-Há (pronounced as 'shell-ha') and Xcaret (pronounced as 'sh-car-et') offer adventures such as exploring underground rivers, cenotes and caves, horseback-riding through forests, snorkelling and swimming with dolphins. Xcaret also has a butterfly pavilion, botanical garden and mushroom farm.

mayan magic

It is here in Quintana Roo that you may begin to see some of the different faces of Mexico's ethnically diverse culture. Originally inhabited by the Maya, ancient people famed for their art, science, architecture and cosmology, it is home to some of the Peninsula's great ceremonial sites.

Between 1000 and 1550 AD (referred to as the post-classic period by historians), the area, now called the Riviera Maya, was an important centre of trading and religious activity for the Mayan civilisation. Its people and trade flourished in the towns of Tulum, Xaman-Há (now called Playa del Carmen), Xcaret and Xel-Há, the first European settlement in the Peninsula.

During the next three centuries, thick vegetation and perennial piracy combined with difficult sea access for large European vessels, prevented this region from being significantly populated until Cancún International Airport made it accessible for locals and tourists in the 1970s.

Despite this long period of abandonment, Mayan culture maintains a strong presence in the state, especially in its architecture and archaeological sites. Besides fishing, windsurfing, kayaking and cenote-diving, visitors can witness the Caribbean

THIS PAGE (FROM TOP): *Encounter nature in the ecological parks and forests of Quintana Roo; the Great Pyramid of Cobá.*
OPPOSITE: *There are over 3,000 cenotes in the Yucatán Peninsula.*

Sea crashing against the pre-Hispanic stones of Tulum, Mexico's beloved seaside ruins, or tread through the mysterious archaeological remains of Cobá, most of which have been left in ruins.

In Yucatán state, and also here in Quintana Roo—where a large proportion of the population is made up of migrants from other parts of Mexico—you may notice the distinctive, regal features of the Mayan people that are startlingly similar to the relief sculptures from the archaeological sites that date back centuries.

Some hotels here have even integrated Mayan customs, language and art into their cultures. Paraíso de la Bonita Resort and Thalasso's architecture features details such as palapa roofs and sunken Mayan bathtubs. Ikal del Mar (Poetry of the Sea in Maya) has a holistic Mayan-style spa, while Maroma Resort and Spa incorporates elaborate Temazcal and star-gazing rituals as part of their activities. Ceiba del Mar Spa Resort's balsamic Mayan massage involves the application of 10 essential oils on your back, followed by hot stone and massage treatments.

cosmopolitan cuisine

In Quintana Roo, the demands and curiosities of different palates have given rise to a multi-ethnic cuisine characterised by dishes that are mostly based on seafood, and complemented by indigenous ingredients. These include achiote (red pulp surrounding the achiote seed, known to some as annatto), used generously in traditional Yucatecan cooking to give dishes like cochinita pibil (pork baked in banana leaves and eaten with soft maize tortillas) a hearty crimson colour.

The area is also known for producing the world's hottest chilli, the yellow habanero—otherwise known as Scotch bonnet pepper or guindilla (its red version)—which is also immensely popular in Jamaica and the Caribbean islands. In Mexico, this is rarely used in the preparation of a dish, but more commonly served on the side as salsa habanero, which is a combination of chilli, red onion, vinegar and oregano. Another fruity but equally feisty chilli from the Yucatán Peninsula is the slightly larger and more orange chile manzana, which is in fact, less dry.

Fresh tropical fruit is typical fare. Citrus fruit such as the naranja agria (sour orange) are common ingredients in chicken and pork marinades, or in sauces for savoury dishes. The lima, a large perfumed lime, is cut into discs and used to flavour the aromatic sopa de lima, a clear broth containing shredded chicken, oregano, onion and strips of fried tortilla. Wonderfully tangy and piquant, this soup is a classic dish of the Peninsula and ideal for the climate.

Quintana Roo caters to all kinds of travellers with an astounding variety of cuisines, including what some call, 'Mayan fusion'. Thanks to the growing influx of tourists, some of the country's best Italian and French restaurants can be found here.

spa drama

Complementing Quintana Roo's gastronomy are some of the country's most inviting spas and North America's only thalassotheraphy centre, which are located within the sleek hotels and resorts of the Riviera Maya. First-time visitors must make it a priority to indulge in the ancient Temazcal (derived from the Náhuatl word,

Temazcalli, which refers to a protected place where the body, mind and spirit are being purified in order for someone to be 'born' again) experience. This ritual is usually conducted in a round, igloo-like hut made of mud, stones or adobe, that represents the womb of mother earth.

A temazcalero leads the guest in an ancient ceremony, which includes cleansing the aura with incense before entering the Temazcal. Herbal water is then poured on the hot stones to produce aromatic steam before the therapist proceeds to rub the body with rosemary, sweet basil and eucalyptus for purification and stimulation. This segment of the ritual is comparable to an elaborate steam bath and massage. The ceremony also includes guided breathing sessions and at times, chanting. It concludes with the application of, or immersion into, cold water to close pores.

The Temazcal ritual is believed to cure illnesses, as its processes help to eliminate toxins, and is an important feature during festivals and celebrations. Still a living tradition in many parts of the country, its physical-spiritual benefits have transcended borders to attract an international following.

THIS PAGE (FROM TOP): A massage at Paraíso de la Bonita Resort and Thalasso includes views of the Caribbean Sea; the hotel's heated thalasso pool.

OPPOSITE (FROM TOP): Cancún's best hotels can be found strung along the Zona Hotelera; over 200 species of fish inhabit the Great Mayan Reef.

bright lights, city sights

Quintana Roo state was created for the sizzling resort city of Cancún, whose high-rise Zona Hotelera (Hotel Zone), built three decades ago, is the success story of a sleepy fishing village. A forgotten mangrove swamp for most of the 19th century, the territory acquired its rather odd name from Mexican dictator Porfirio Díaz in 1902, honouring his army general, Andrés Quintana Roo. But it wasn't granted statehood until Cancún opened for business and development in 1974.

Today's Cancún is glitzy, polished and bursting with life. Clean, organised and safe, this cosmopolitan city thrives with beaches that are known for their pure white, powdery sand and a cityscape that is packed with trendy bars, classy restaurants, world-class golf courses, grand hotels, sprawling shopping-cum-entertainment complexes and towering office blocks. The bright colours of its ocean-front buildings are set against the shimmering tones of the sea that

intensify from a dazzling turquoise to deep sapphire, adding a picture-perfect appeal to an already irresistible resort setting.

The Zona Hotelera is actually a 14-mile (22-km) barrier island shaped like the number seven, and divided principally from the mainland by Laguna Nichupte. At the northeastern tip, the Cancún Convention Centre is a popular venue for cultural events. It also houses the Instituto Nacional de Antropología e Historia (National Institute of Anthropology and History), a small museum which focuses on the area's Mayan culture. Guided tours are available in most European languages.

Next to the centre lies Coral Negro, an open-air market specialising in local crafts, while west along Boulevard Kukulcán lies a half-mile (1-km) strip of shopping malls. Kukulcán Plaza houses over 100 shops and designer boutiques as well as a bowling alley and video arcade. While Cancún can be pricey, its duty-free stores such as Ultrafemme in Kukulcán Plaza offer designer products, perfume and jewellery at significantly reduced rates.

South of the Cancún Convention Centre lies Las Ruinas del Rey, dated from 200 to 300 BC. The past meets the present in this ancient Mayan structure nestled right in the middle of the Zona Hotelera. This is the largest ruin in town and said to have been a royal burial ground. Excavated in the 1950s, it is now part of a beach-and-golf resort complex.

THIS PAGE (FROM LEFT): *Seven out of eight endangered species of sea turtles reside in Mexican waters; yachts from all over the world dock at Isla Mujeres for sailfishing tournaments.*

OPPOSITE (FROM TOP): *The heavenly blue expanse of Isla Mujeres; with coral reefs just off the shore, scuba diving is naturally the biggest sport on the island.*

Within the zone, you'll also find Cancún's wildest discos and salsa clubs such as La Boom, The Bull Dog Café, Dady'O, Azucar and Batacha. In autumn, the city plays host to the Mexican and Caribbean music and dance festival, while the annual jazz festival is a major international event that lasts a week in late May. Boats, helicopters, marinas, water-themed parks and entertainment centres such as Aqua World, Aqua Fun, El Embarcadero (for the Aquabus and captain Hook Galleon) and Parque Nizuk line the area, together with boat charters for deep-sea fishing and scuba diving. The main 18-hole golf course, Pok-Ta-Pok, offers golfers unparalleled views of both the sea and lagoon.

fantasy islands

Unlike Cancún, Isla Mujeres is relatively peaceful and some have joked that the island is perfect for those who prefer siestas to nightclubs. But being just across from Cancún—whose lights shine upon the island like a huge cruise ship—all of the city's action is merely 20 minutes away by speedboat.

Still relatively undeveloped, this compact limestone island is a little gem measuring only 6 sq miles (16 sq km). You can easily travel around it in a rented golf cart, moped or bicycle. It was named Isla Mujeres (Island of Women) when 16th-century Spanish explorers landed and found clay female figurines in a temple dedicated to Ix Chel (Mayan goddess of the moon and fertility).

There are plenty of water activities such as drift diving and snorkelling. The island's west side is a protected zone, containing the Garrafón Underwater Park, a landscape of corals and reefs bursting with life and colour. It is also a site for turtles and seabirds. An educational marine aquarium, the Isla Mujeres Turtle Farm is also a hatching ground for the endangered turtles. Here, hatchlings are raised in captivity, then released back into the sea.

Divers can visit the Cave of the Sleeping Sharks, where a mixture of salt and freshwater makes the resident nurse sharks groggy and slow. Other attractions include Mardi Gras (Carnival), which is celebrated for one week in February.

The island has long played host to two sailing regattas that call for a week of festivities each spring. During this time, multi-million-dollar fishing boats and yachts from North Carolina, Florida and Texas dock here to participate in these world-class sport fishing tournaments.

Some of Isla Mujeres' best hotels offer their guests the thrill of marlin fishing from custom-built boats, under the supervision of experienced crew. Guests will have a chance to catch kingfish, white and blue marlin, dorado, blackfin tuna and more. Bird lovers can take a 45-minute boat ride up north to Isla Contoy, a neighbouring Caribbean island and sanctuary for hundreds of bird species such as cranes, pelicans, pintail ducks and spoonbills.

In fact, the entire state of Quintana Roo is a haven for bird lovers who flock to Sian Ka'an to see the quetzal, macaw and harpy eagle. About 345 local species, ranging from varieties of parrot, toucan, hummingbird, falcon and pheasant, to over 1,000 species of migratory birds live here.

stylish strands

For a change of scene, those looking for a fashionable venue now head southwards, away from Cancún to the Riviera Maya. Only 20 miles (32 km) south of Cancún airport, this dreamy coastline stretches from Puerto Morelos down to Punto Allen inside the Sian Ka'an Biosphere Reserve. Its largest communities are Playa del Carmen, Puerto Aventuras, Akumal and Tulum.

Since 1998, the Riviera Maya has grown fast, attracting heads of state and the rich and famous, as Acapulco did in its heyday. But this time, state authorities have recognised that one of the Riviera's greatest appeals lies in the exclusivity of its white beaches and set out to preserve the magical combination of powdery coral sand, swaying palms and complete privacy.

Far removed from Cancún's urbanity, resorts in the Riviera nevertheless benefit from the town's infrastructure, including the international airport and the best road in the republic—the Cancún-Tulum highway.

More and more visitors are beginning to appreciate the fishing village ambience of Puerto Morelos and its convenient location between Cancún and Playa del Carmen, using it as a base for discovering Quintana Roo.

Playa del Carmen, despite being the largest town on the Riviera, is laid-back and friendly. Often referred to as 'Playa', it exudes a stylish European character of its own. Only 40 miles (63 km) south of Cancún, its relaxed ambience is a welcome contrast to the former's fast-paced lifestyle. And it doesn't fall short of amenities as shops and boutiques here sell everything including handmade pottery, art, handicrafts, beachwear and jewellery.

Playa has the buzz of a tropical seaside town, where people-watching is a regular pastime. As the day progresses, the locals can be seen walking their dogs, or setting up tables outdoors to play chess and cards, sipping on anything from cassis to cappuccino to piña coladas. On a typical evening, the seductive aromas of seafood waft through Quinta Avenida (Fifth Avenue), signalling the time for dinner at any of its stylish restaurants.

THIS PAGE: *Powder-white sand and luminous water are the defining traits of Riviera Maya's strands.*

OPPOSITE (FROM TOP): *The calm, clear water of the Great Mayan Reef is ideal for snorkelling; Playa del Carmen's sexy beaches are a magnet for the rich, famous and beautiful.*

Dancing is also a serious affair in Playa's nightlife. Mambo Café throbs with salsa and Latin beats, while the ultra cool Los Aluxes spins house music inside a natural cave. But the air-conditioned Cancún- style discos are carefully avoided because dancing by the shore is considered a lot groovier.

underwater world

Just a 45-minute ferry ride from Playa's pier is Cozumel, Mexico's largest island covering an area of 5,274 sq ft (490 sq km). Surrounded by turquoise sea, Cozumel is renowned for its warm, crystal clear water and incredible marine life, which can be viewed at the Palancar National Underwater Park.

This forms part of the Great Mayan Reef, which starts in Cabo Catoche at the north of Quintana Roo and skirts the coasts of Belize, Guatemala and Honduras. Also known as the Mesoamerican Reef, it is extremely deep in parts, and the water's transparency lets in light that is essential to coral growth.

The Mexican part of the reef measures 186 miles (300 km) and the water surrounding Cozumel is so clear that visibility extends up to 250 ft (61m). It was the site of numerous studies done by oceanographer Jacques Cousteau, and in 1980, its western coast was declared a sanctuary for marine flora and fauna.

Among sea horses, turtles, moray eels and lobsters, over 200 species of tropical fish, including the blue-and-yellow queen angelfish and the rare toadfish, can be seen here. Cozumel is today considered the best scuba-diving location in the western hemisphere and one of the top five in the world.

Another beautiful spot south of the island is Chankanaab Lagoon, which is linked to the sea via natural caverns. Its shallow coral formations are just under 30 ft (9 m), making it the world's only inland reef. Experience drift diving at Punta Sur, Palancar and Maracaibo, or explore the Mayan ruins set in the gardens of Chankanaab National Park. Golfers can also visit Cozumel Country Club for the 18-hole golf course which is regarded as one of the most spectacular in the Caribbean. With all these activities in store, there is never a lack of things to do in Cozumel.

THIS PAGE (FROM TOP): Visual entertainment at Deseo [Hotel + Lounge]; windsurfing adventures abound in Cozumel where sailboats can be hired anywhere.
OPPOSITE: The hotel's sleek bar by the pool is the meeting place for Playa's stylish set.

Ceiba del Mar Spa Resort

Ceiba del Mar Spa Resort has perfected the formula for a 'healthy' holiday—lots of undisturbed rest, sun, good food and the option of working out in a modern gym. It offers an amazing myriad of spa treatments that can hardly be considered 'hard work'. Choose to be massaged and caressed into a state of semi-consciousness in their deluxe spa or beneath their Mayan palapa-thatched pavilions by the sea.

Ideally situated along the Riviera Maya and coddled between turquoise Caribbean waters and tropical forests, the resort has 120 luxury rooms and six plush suites to ensure you will never need to jostle for attention. It maintains an intimate atmosphere and offers impeccable service. And even then, the rooms are spaciously set apart in eight buildings that are just three stories high.

The feel is distinctively provincial even though you're just minutes away from the buzzing town of Cancún. Making your way from your room to the beach, restaurant, spa or tennis court requires you to meander through gardens of manicured tropical plants. This is a sheer delight in itself.

Contemporary Mexican in style, natural elements such as granite stone accents and thatched-roof buildings, designed by architect Luis Segura, add to the village atmosphere. But that's where all references to the provincial way of life end.

Rooms are thoroughly modern. Awash with the cheerful shades characteristic of the country, all are equipped with conveniences such as cable television and data ports that keep the rest of the world at your fingertips. There's also a jacuzzi with sunroof in each of the eight buildings, giving you more venues

THIS PAGE: Rooms and suites offer views of the pool or the sparkling waters of the Caribbean.

OPPOSITE (FROM TOP): Merely minutes from Cancún, the luxurious resort offers easy access to city conveniences and the tranquillity of a beachside village; dazzling sunset views from the pool deck.

to bask in the sun besides the two large swimming pools and beach.

Most people embark on a spa holiday expecting to starve. At Ceiba del Mar, you're free to do so, but it would be such a pity with all the delectable food available. There's El Arrecife, a bar and grill by the beach that's popular for lunch with its selection of choice seafood from the area, and Xtabay, which offers delicious spa meals using only the freshest ingredients, vegetables and exotic fruit. In fact, it is assumed that guests should have a healthy appetite. After all, the first meal of the day is delivered with coffee and tea to all rooms and suites through a butler box.

But it must be said that the star of Ceiba del Mar is still the spa. With a state-of-the-art fitness centre, sauna, steam bath and plunge pool sprawled over 8,611 sq ft (800 sq m) of space, it is easily the largest in the area. Cardiovascular exercise is available through trained instructors for gymnasium enthusiasts, or you could keep fit with yoga or tai chi lessons held on the beach.

The full-service spa offers the whole gamut of treatments from facials that treat sun-burnt skin to massages that ease away

jet lag. With European efficiency and Mexican hospitality, it attracts patrons from the nearby cities of Cancún and Playa del Carmen as well. Especially popular and exclusive to Ceiba del Mar's spa is the Temazcal treatment—a traditional ritual held in a terra cotta hut by the beach at sunset.

Considered to have purifying effects on both mind and body, the Temazcal experience involves being 'cleansed' by hot volcanic rocks enhanced with aromatic herbs, then massaged with thick aloe vera slabs. It is a treatment traditionally used by young Mayan couples before their weddings as

THIS PAGE (CLOCKWISE FROM TOP LEFT): Yoga lessons in a beachfront, Mayan-style pavilion; rose petal-filled jacuzzi; tai chi for stress reduction and balance of mind and body; one of the resort's two glamorous pools.

OPPOSITE (FROM LEFT): Fine dining at El Arecife restaurant; each of the eight hotel buildings is fitted with a rooftop jacuzzi.

it symbolises the act of being 'reborn'. These exceptional treatments are available throughout the year and offer holistic healing for guests seeking alternative routes to their wellbeing. You can choose to balance your chakras, view your aura or open your energy centres with a trained naturopathic healer.

Ceiba del Mar's approach to healthy living clearly strives to reduce stress and incorporate balance, which is why everything here seems effortless and pleasurable. You'll realise at the end of your stay that the toughest thing you'll need to do at Ceiba del Mar is to leave.

PHOTOGRAPHS COURTESY OF CEIBA DEL MAR SPA RESORT.

FACTS

ROOMS	120 rooms • 6 suites
FOOD	El Arrecife: international • Xtabay: spa cuisine
DRINK	2 bars
FEATURES	spa with full aromatherapy and holistic services • sauna • steam room • 2 pools • gym • Swiss showers • tennis court • 8 rooftop jacuzzis • book, CD and video library
BUSINESS	multi-function room with audio-visual equipment • data port in all rooms
NEARBY	2 golf courses • Xcaret and Xel-há ecological parks • Playa del Carmen • Cancún
CONTACT	Costera Norte, Lote 1, Smz 10, Puerto Morelos, Quintana Roo 77580 • telephone: +52.998 872 8060 • facsimile: +52.998 872 8061 • email: reserve@ceibadelmar.com • website: www.ceibadelmar.com

Deseo [Hotel + Lounge]

If you think Playa del Carmen is all about white beaches, beautiful bodies and dusk-till-dawn beach raves, you're probably right. And now, there's another reason to head for this stretch of beach south of Cancún, with the opening of Deseo [Hotel + Lounge].

The feel of this exclusive 15-room retreat, however, is decidedly more cosmopolitan chic than surfer hip. Far from the staid Caribbean formula of terra cotta and tiles, its charm is reflected through its crisp white-and-aqua design, theatrical drapes, piped-in ambient music, and extravagant use of beige marble and dark wood.

Logs become balcony railings, while straw hats, carry-alls, flip-flops and bananas are threaded through wires and suspended from the ceiling as ready-made art. With Deseo's cool Philippe Starck aesthetic, it is easy to forget that you're living it up in what was formerly a rural fishing town.

Despite its luxurious trappings, the heart of Deseo ('desire' in Spanish) is young and funky. Urbanites come here for the cool

atmosphere, ideal weather and none of the formality of other large-scale establishments. Activities at the hotel, located on Playa's main road, are centred around the bar, lounge and pool deck, where lithe bodies tan on oversized daybeds, and party beneath the stars by night.

There is certainly much going on in the courtyard of this two-storey resort. Rooms are converted into living rooms for daytime socialising, while the pool deck transforms into a hip lounge where a DJ keeps the crowd entertained. This is the ultimate meeting place where the pretty folk of Playa come out to play—dancing to club beats to the sound of crashing waves.

But even with the pristine beaches beckoning, you won't be leaving your room fast enough to ignore the little details included within. Handmade soaps, fluffy rugs, lavish white sheets and king-size beds tempt you to linger in your room just a little longer. The suites come with spectacular views of the ocean, complete with your very own open-air bathtub.

Whichever room you choose, be it a room with a terrace or one overlooking the swimming pool, all have access to the beach, just a two-minute walk away. Creative touches include hammocks in all

Step outside of Deseo and you'll find yourself in the centre of everything that is happening on Quinta Avenida (Fifth Avenue). Chic dining, designer shopping and Mexican-Caribbean-style nightlife are some adventures that Playa has to offer.

With carefully bronzed bodies at every corner, the scene at Deseo sizzles in more ways than one. Even the hotel staff—hip and international—are worth more than a second glance.

Deseo is dedicated to the louche lifestyle of lounging and there's no better time to do so than when the sun is up. Be it by the pool with other glamorous guests, in the outdoor jacuzzi or on a hammock in the privacy of your room, sun-basking options are aplenty here.

The food too, is dedicated to the youthful lifestyle of Deseo. There are no lengthy dégustation menus or endless breakfast buffet tables when guests are still recovering from the previous night's excesses. In fact, there is no restaurant. But what it does serve from its self-service kitchen are tapas, complimentary health snacks and American breakfasts. However, Deseo makes up for its lack in cuisine with a well-stocked beverage department. Once the music picks up, the bartender shifts into high

THIS PAGE: *Deseo's sparkling pool is Playa's hottest hang-out.*

OPPOSITE (CLOCKWISE FROM LEFT): *Giant sunbeds for basking and socialising in the day or at night; the pool bar comes complete with plush towels and cocktails; imaginative wall art raises the level of beach chic; tapas and snacks are served from the self-service kitchen.*

rooms and a novel party kit containing incense and condoms for each guest.

You won't forget for a moment that you're in the Caribbean, where the beaches are busy but beautiful, and the sand feels like silk on your skin. Deseo's location, some 35 miles (56 km) south of Cancún on the Mayan Riviera, offers the prettiest coastline. With its white beaches, crystal clear waters and exotic wildlife, the Riviera Maya is a playground that is hard to beat.

...even with the pristine beaches beckoning, you won't be leaving your room fast enough...

gear, serving up a mean selection of cocktails to go with the Spanish bites.

Conceived by the people who own HABITA and Hotel Condesa in Mexico City, Deseo incorporates the natural elements of the Yucatán Peninsula to offer guests a unique perspective of the beach resort.

With the area's splendid beaches and untouched beauty, it is not without reason that Mexico's Pacific Coast has attracted some of the world's most famous, high-luxury hotel groups to its shores.

So when in Deseo, forget about resting. Come here to party hard.

FACTS

ROOMS	12 rooms • 3 suites
FOOD	self-service kitchen: tapas, snacks and American breakfasts
DRINK	poolside bar
FEATURES	pool • lounge • jacuzzi • library
BUSINESS	Internet access
NEARBY	beaches • coral reefs • restaurants • designer shops • bars • cafés
CONTACT	5a Avenida Y Calle 12, Playa del Carmen, Quintana Roo 77710 • telephone: +52.984 879 3620 • facsimile: +52.984 879 3621 • email: info@hoteldeseo.com • website: www.hoteldeseo.com

PHOTOGRAPHS BY JEAN-LUC LALOUX AND UNDINE PRÖHL (BATHTUB AND WALL FEATURE), COURTESY OF DESEO [HOTEL + LOUNGE].

Ikal del Mar

Those who would like to play along the Playa del Carmen stretch but prefer to sleep away from it should stay at Ikal del Mar, an intimate, 30-bungalow hotel situated just 10 miles (16 km) north of the party zone. Despite this proximity, Ikal del Mar seems worlds away, nestled in a clearing at the edge of a primitive Mayan jungle and embraced by an isolated strip of Caribbean beach.

Nothing seems to disturb the solitude of the place, save for the waking of tropical birds in the morning. Cleverly woven into the dense jungle, Ikal del Mar seems not to exist. The almost virgin jungle remains mostly untouched: old trees are respected and villas are built around them, while new saplings are allowed to thrive on the meandering paths. The obtrusive noise and pollution of motorised vehicles are also deliberately kept at bay. In the evenings, stars viewed from the hotel seem to sparkle more brightly as your gaze is undistracted by the glare of electric lights. Torches, instead, dimly light the way.

While these are all worthy efforts by the developers to live within the jungle without disturbing it, for guests, it makes for an unforgettably tranquil and surreal experience. What's more, Ikal del Mar manages to accomplish all this with five-star aplomb. Rooms are self-contained villas, comprising of a large room and platform bed dressed with romantic draped netting. Bathrooms are

THIS PAGE (CLOCKWISE FROM TOP): *The resort's eco-conscious concept has found a following among nature-loving travellers; the spa menu features treatments such as the raindrop massage which purportedly eases away back problems; guests can lounge by the pool and admire the beach.*

OPPOSITE: *Villas come complete with private pools, outdoor showers and terraces with hammocks.*

glamorous and spacious, with an outdoor shower in the back garden. And then there is the front patio that's so stylish and comfortable, you'd be tempted to spend the rest of your stay here. There's a plunge pool, terry-covered chaises, and a hand-woven hammock—all within a pristine setting of white walls and floor.

Beyond the grounds of the hotel lies the beach: a gleaming white strip coddled by jungle and azure waters. An infinity pool offers the best views of the beach, while Azul, the main restaurant makes the most of its beautiful surroundings with outdoor dining options. Gourmet Mexican cuisine inspired by feisty Mesoamerican flavours, is the speciality of this fine dining restaurant. Casual meals can be had at The Grill by the poolside, where the not-to-be-missed lobster club sandwich is served.

If you're still in the mood for over-the-top pampering, visit Ikal del Mar's spa for a speciality massage which involves kneading by the sea followed by the delicious slathering of Mayan mud, herbal clay and essential oils—all indigenous ingredients of the area. The spa also offers a range of holistic healing treatments, including the traditional Temazcal, a Mesoamerican-style sweat bath that has purification benefits. At Ikal del Mar, being ecofriendly has never been a more luxurious affair.

PHOTOGRAPHS COURTESY OF IKAL DEL MAR.

FACTS		
ROOMS	29 villas • 1 presidential villa
FOOD	Azul: Mesoamerican • The Grill: poolside dining
DRINK	Bar at Azul: cocktails, desserts and snacks
FEATURES	jungle surroundings • ecofriendly concept • spa • pool • private beach
BUSINESS	event and meeting facilities
NEARBY	golf course • Playa del Carmen • Xcaret ecological park • Cozumel • Mérida city • Tulum and Uxmal ruins
CONTACT	Playa Xcalacoco, Riviera Maya, Quintana Roo 77710 • telephone: +52.713 528 7863 • facsimile: +52.713 528 3697 • email: reservations@ikaldelmar.com • website: www.ikaldelmar.com

Maroma Resort + Spa

The fantasy of running off to an unspoiled and isolated beach paradise has always been particularly beguiling. But the problem for today's escapists is that paradise is easily spoiled by their arrival. First, an airstrip, then beach cabanas, jet-skis, a hotel, a casino, and before you know it, you can't even see the sand. Fortunately, there's an alternative in Maroma Resort and Spa, a luxurious hideaway situated on one of the world's best beaches, and protected by 200 acres (81 hectares) of jungle reserve. The place is so eco-sensitive and landscape-appropriate, it seems to disappear into the scenery. Surprisingly, this discreet spot is just 30 miles (48 km) south of Cancún, but it remains miles away from the city's brisk pace and lifestyle.

The Maroma experience begins the moment you search for it. There are no signages on the left turn off the highway, and don't be surprised when a smiling guard greets you by name when you arrive at the gatekeeper's lodge. Then it's a bumpy, 15-minute drive through a jungle

THIS PAGE (CLOCKWISE FROM TOP): Daytime activities are centred around the sprawling pool; sitting on the edge of the Caribbean, Maroma's villas are fronted by natural beauty; buildings crafted by hand feature carved niches, stone walls and water fountains.

OPPOSITE (FROM TOP): Guests can look forward to stretches of unspoiled beach and jungle; ancient sculptures reflect the resort's strong Mayan traditions.

before Maroma's white stucco walls and thatched turrets appear.

As only a tenth of its sprawling 25-acre (10-hectare) land is developed in order to preserve ecological balance, guests have unlimited space to roam and explore. A labyrinth of paths lined with terra cotta pots leads guests through a landscape of lush palms and tropical jungle flowers. Colourful butterflies flit among the shrubs, exotic parrots perch on branches, and peacocks prance around quite freely. The crowning attraction, a 750-ft (229-m) private stretch of beach, is flanked by the Caribbean's blue waters and natural vegetation of sea-grape trees, coconut palms and hibiscus.

Following its philosophy of 'handmade hospitality', construction of Maroma's villas, which house 65 guestrooms, was entirely machine-free. Eco-conscious guests will be delighted to learn that every building on the property has been made by hand, without any machinery or electricity.

The blueprint of the buildings was drawn on sand, and within weeks, the building blocks were expertly pieced together by skilled masons. Corners were finished off by chisel, walls stuccoed by hand, and timber pillars shaped by machetes. Even the exquisite rugs by the beds were woven by women from a nearby village.

The effect is homely, residential and natural, like sharing a bit of paradise with a couple of friends. Unsurprisingly, it was exactly how the resort had evolved. The piece of land on which Maroma now sits was

...a miniature Eden of Moorish-Mayan huts hidden in a dense tropical jungle.

THIS PAGE: *Enjoy a book beneath the swaying palms, or head for the beach, just steps ahead.*

OPPOSITE (CLOCKWISE FROM LEFT): *A canopy bed, mahogany furniture and fine paintings exude a Moorish feel; bathrooms are resplendent with sunken tubs and hand-painted tiles; the Temazcal's ancient Mayan cleansing ritual is a must-try for tired guests.*

chanced upon by architect and founder José Luis Moreno 30 years ago. He envisioned a home, and someday, a boutique hotel edged by nature's perfection. He then embarked on attaining his dream when he met his wife Sally Shaw who shared his vision.

Over 15 years, the original house on the beach grew bit-by-bit, room-by-room, without electricity or heavy machinery and always with the jungle intact. Along the way, they shared their home with friends from around the world. Today, guests, treated like friends, are immersed in a miniature Eden of Moorish-Mayan huts hidden in a dense tropical jungle.

Luxury does co-exist splendidly with nature in this ecofriendly resort. Simple and unpretentious materials such as the salmon-coloured stones from a nearby quarry are favoured over fancy marble. But here, they are so intricately embedded with shell fossils, they glint and sparkle under the moonlight.

Rooms glow with the warmth of mahogany wood and bamboo, and outside, a large terrace beckons with a hammock. The oversized bathrooms are resplendent with colourful hand-painted tiles lining the walls, mammoth tubs, Roman-style open showers and deliciously thick towels. The setting here is so idyllic and luxurious, guests will want to enjoy it all in secluded serenity.

There are, however, plenty of activities to entice guests to venture out of their rooms. The new Mayan-themed spa offers saltwater

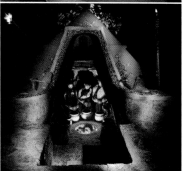

flotation and massage treatment rooms, and one really shouldn't leave without trying the Temazcal—a cleansing ritual that takes place in an ancient sweat lodge.

At the rustically elegant El Sol, Mayan-Yucatecan cuisine with a touch of French classicism is served. Dinner is a languorous and romantic affair at this indoor-outdoor restaurant, where guests can enjoy the sea breeze and ocean, amid a setting of fine china and crystal. The addition of two state-of-the-art kitchens has also inspired the creation of Cilantro, a health bar for light meals and snacks to complement the spa.

What's best about Maroma, however, is its unfailing discretion. Secretive and discrete, it whispers rather than shouts luxury. And it is notoriously hard to find. Which means that when you do finally arrive at its grounds, you'll feel like you've chanced upon your own little bit of paradise.

FACTS	
ROOMS	65 rooms
FOOD	El Sol: European-inspired Mayan-Yucatecan • Cilantro: health bar
DRINK	Maroma Bar • beach bar
FEATURES	3 pools • 2 tennis courts • spa • jacuzzi • wellness centre • Temazcal
BUSINESS	meeting and banquet facilities
NEARBY	Chichén Itzá, Cobá, Tulum and Uxmal ruins • Sian Ka'an Biosphere Reserve • Great Mayan Reef • Cozumel • Isla Contoy • Cancún • Playa del Carmen
CONTACT	Highway 307, Riviera Maya km 51, Quintana Roo 77710 • telephone: +52.998 872 8200 • facsimile: +52.998 872 8220 • email: reservations@maromahotel.com • website: www.maromahotel.com

PHOTOGRAPHS COURTESY OF MAROMA RESORT + SPA.

Mosquito Blue

If your idea of an ideal holiday is limitless sun, endless white beaches, and long nights of non-stop partying, you've come to no better place than Playa del Carmen, the seaside venue for the world's most enthusiastic sun- and fun-seekers. Fortunately, despite its popularity, Playa's miles of beaches remain alabaster white, its waters teeming with colourful marine life, and its charm unfaded. In fact, residents of Playa attribute its unique vagabond traveller ambience to the large number of foreign visitors that party on its shores.

If it's this carefree holiday ambience that you crave, and yet are apprehensive about facing the crowds, stay at Mosquito Blue, the small boutique resort that's situated in the heart of Playa, but offers privacy should you

THIS PAGE (CLOCKWISE FROM TOP):
All rooms have easy access to the hotel's two large pools; Mosquito Blue sits on a landscape of lush greenery; an Asian feel is created with Indonesian furnishing.
OPPOSITE: The main building's palapa-thatched roof brings the beach feel into the hotel.

need it. Overlooking a busy pedestrian plaza, guests only need step out to experience all that the village is famous for: vibrant cafés and restaurants, and rows of stalls selling Mexican arts and crafts. The popular beach with the requisite bronzed sun worshippers is just a short walk away.

And yet, at times when solitude is a luxury, guests may seek refuge at the hotel's fern-filled courtyard or on the terraces in their rooms. Of the 47 rooms, the ones closest to the courtyard are the most peaceful; most offer views of the lush gardens and the two swimming pools.

Pared-down luxury best describes the décor of the rooms. Intimate and cosy, the walls are washed in the hotel's signature colours of yellow and blue, and the beds are carved in dark mahogany. Offering one of the most glamorous bathrooms in town, the showers and floors here are extravagantly laid with marble.

What's most striking, however, is the youthful, vivacious air of Playa that pervades the hotel: the lobby, modern and minimalist, resembles an art gallery with paintings by local artists decorating its walls; it also features a curving staircase and open-air bar. Ethnic Asian touches can be found throughout the hotel with Indonesian furniture and decorative elements.

Glass Bar, an Italian restaurant and wine bar, is pretty much the focal point of Mosquito Blue and its night scene. With a cellar that features over 10,000 bottles of wine, it has one of the largest and finest selections of Italian wines in Playa, and has become a trendy spot for guests who converge for inventive meals, drinks, socialising and people-watching.

The energetic vibe of Playa is undeniable, and at Mosquito Blue, you can now enjoy all the sun-filled adventures it has to offer in high luxury.

FACTS

ROOMS	46 rooms • 1 suite
FOOD	Glass Bar: haute Italian
DRINK	Blue Bar
FEATURES	2 pools • gym • snooker table • dive shop
BUSINESS	Internet access • event and meeting facilities
NEARBY	beach • beach bar • Tulum, Chichén Itzá and Uxmal ruins
CONTACT	Quinta Avenida Entre 12 to 14 , Playa del Carmen, Quintana Roo 77710 • telephone: +52.984 873 1335 • facsimile: +52.984 873 1337 • email: information@mosquitoblue.com • website: www.mosquitoblue.com

PHOTOGRAPHS COURTESY OF MOSQUITO BLUE.

Na Balam

Situated on an island so small that you could easily get around on a bicycle or golf cart, Na Balam is just the kind of place you'd imagine a writer retreating to for weeks at a time to bash away at a typewriter in complete isolation. In fact, this hotel on Isla Mujeres, a 20-minute boat ride from Cancún, is fast becoming known as a haven for those seeking an introspective vacation, such as yoga teachers and students who come here for its serenity and flawless beaches.

With endless palms swaying in the tropical breeze, and the sandy white beach of Playa Norte within easy access, Na Balam is a sensuous, laid-back retreat from the heady experience that's so much a part of Mexico.

THIS PAGE (CLOCKWISE FROM TOP): The spa provides guests with plenty of tempting options for body-pampering treatments; the island's tranquillity is a major draw for travellers seeking peace and serenity; a private plunge pool offers inspiring views of the sea.

OPPOSITE: Evenings are torch-lit events where guests find their way to the hotel's restaurant and bar by flickering lights.

...rooms are spread out over an expanse of tropical gardens in quaint two-storey cottages...

Na Balam stands out in Isla Mujeres' accommodation menu as a singularly luxurious hotel with all the amenities and furnishings tailored to international travellers. And yet, with its breezy and casual architecture, it maintains the charming local flavour of Isla Mujeres.

Thirty-one rooms are spread out over an expanse of tropical gardens in quaint two-storey cottages that very much resemble the residences of the native islanders. Rooms are large, airy and cool, dressed in varying shades of white and ecru. Terraces and balconies allow guests proximity to the ocean which can be admired from every room, and a hammock adds to the island-life ambience. The effect is infinitely calming.

The unhurried pace of the island attracts yoga enthusiasts who come to Na Balam for a spot of undisturbed meditation on its beach. There is also a spa on the grounds for even more solitary pleasures.

The island, however, offers a wide range of activities for the more boisterous: cycling is the first choice for getting around, and ideal for familiarising yourself with the place and the friendly islanders. There's also an endless list of aqua activities, including swimming with the dolphins in the crystalline waters of the five-and-a-half-mile- (nine-km-) long island.

In the evenings, guests can head for Zazil Ha, one of Isla Mujeres' most popular restaurants—a romantic villa where guests dine by candlelight under a thatched-palapa roof. The menu is an eclectic mix of Mayan cooking and European favourites, presenting a fusion of flavours. Snack Bar by the beach, on the other hand, is the place for fruit juices. A casual joint serving light seafood fare, it offers unbeatable views of the sunset, or if you wake up early enough, glorious sunrises that seem to belong only to you.

FACTS		
	ROOMS	28 standard rooms • 3 deluxe master suites
	FOOD	Zazil Ha: fusion • Snack Bar: Mexican snacks and seafood
	DRINK	Zazil Ha • Snack Bar: fresh fruit juices
	FEATURES	rooms with terraces or balconies in standalone cottages • pool • meditation room • yoga on the beach
	BUSINESS	meeting room • Internet access
	NEARBY	Cancún • Isla Contoy • Cave of the Sleeping Sharks (dive site)
	CONTACT	Calle Zazil Ha 118, Playa Norte, Isla Mujeres, Quintana Roo 77400 • telephone: +52.998 877 0279 • facsimile: +52.998 877 0446 • email: nabalam@nabalam.com • website: www.nabalam.com

PHOTOGRAPHS COURTESY OF NA BALAM.

Paraíso de la Bonita Resort + Thalasso

No longer are the world's most fastidious spa goers restricting their holidays to the European Alps and lakes. These days, they need look no further than Asia and America for some of the most luxurious and exclusive spa hotels. The coast of Mexico, for one, has been gaining a reputation for providing the unbeatable spa experience—luxury combined with a real commitment to beauty and wellbeing. Impeccably white beaches, turquoise waters, jade foliage, coupled with the friendly and hospitable nature of the Mexicans, all add to a vacation that far surpasses the regular retreats.

And when it comes to the ideal location for a restful getaway, it's hard to beat Petenpich Bay—an isolated stretch of powder-white beach along the Riviera Maya that is flanked by the Mediterranean Sea and lush jungle. It is also home to the 90-room Paraíso de la Bonita Resort and Thalasso, one of the most stunning hotels in this part of the world. This property scores high on the indulgence scale, and yet provides clinical expertise in its thalassotherapy spa, the first of its kind in Mexico.

Managed by the InterContinental group, Paraíso de la Bonita, which aptly means 'paradise of beautiful women', undulates along a long crest of unspoiled beach, 12 miles (19 km) south from Cancún's international airport. Despite its proximity to the bustling town, the hotel starts at least a mile (2 km) from the main road through a dense jungle that filters out the noise, stress and pollution. The village of haciendas that one finally arrives at is tranquil, with traditional Yucatán architecture that advocates laid-back casualness.

Here, you'll realise that city-style glamour is best left to the cities, and appreciate the simplicity of its thatched roofs, cedar-beamed ceilings, traditional ironwork and colonial archways. The beauty of the place is more pretty than grand, with intricate mosaic pathways leading to small open courtyards.

Though the hotel's architecture is distinctly Mexican, each suite strives to be different, taking on different themes—African, Balinese, Caribbean, Indian and Asian—with fabrics, furnishings and artefacts gathered from the travels of the hotel's owner. The most pervasive of all is its ornamental Asian influence. The elegant dining room of the suites for example, features a beautifully handcrafted marble table resting on Balinese lion heads.

Ground-floor rooms feature plunge pools, while guests on the upper level can enjoy a spacious outdoor terrace with a sun lounge or hammock, complemented by views of the sparkling Caribbean. While the rest of the hotel adopts a rather rustic

THIS PAGE: Paraíso de la Bonita houses Mexico's only thalassotherapy spa.

OPPOSITE (FROM TOP): The reception area with its indigenous architecture, overlooks the outdoor pool; each suite is richly accented with a colonial archway, and Mayan-inspired details.

THIS PAGE (CLOCKWISE FROM RIGHT):
Magnificent views of the ocean from the outdoor terrace; the spa's Mayan-style jacuzzi uses high-pressured seawater to invigorate the body; La Canoa, one of three dining rooms in the resort, specialises in seafood creations.

OPPOSITE: *The resort is just a few steps away from the Caribbean.*

approach with unfinished walls and exposed hand-hewn timber, it's in the bathrooms that luxury becomes unrestrained. Large en-suite bathrooms pamper with cool unpolished marble, deep marble bathtubs, separate showers and handcrafted sinks.

However, the bathrooms are just one option for getting comfortably wet at Paraíso de la Bonita. There is the serene and large reflective outdoor pool—as much an architectural aesthetic as a functional

facility—that forms the centre of the property, or the jacuzzi, steam saunas and plunge pools at the hotel's spa. And make no mistake about this spa and its impressive facilities. It is mammoth at 22,000 sq ft (2,044 sq m)—a sprawling temple of spa delights with heavy stone walls, enveloped by cool air. It may look like an ancient Greek bath, but it is actually equipped with hi-tech facilities. There are high-pressure jet showers, a Mayan-style jacuzzi, steam and dry

saunas, and 17 treatment rooms, offering almost anything from a traditional Swedish massage to New Age reiki.

The speciality of the place, however, is thalassotherapy, an ancient technique that uses heated seawater and mineral-rich marine algae to massage the body so as to ease arthritis and aid circulation. It has been recognised as a legitimate health treatment by Europeans for decades.

Offered for the first time in Mexico at Paraíso de la Bonita, it is applied with strict medical supervision by a group of in-house doctors. Besides its curative benefits, there is also the relaxation aspect—nothing beats sitting back in the warm seawater of the outdoor thalassotherapy pool.

Paraíso de la Bonita's discreet luxury and expert spa therapies as well as its beautiful beach and jungle will attract not only the most fervent spa seekers, but anyone looking for a perfect getaway.

FACTS		
ROOMS	90 suites	
FOOD	The Restaurant: international • Grill: grilled meats and fish • La Canoa: seafood	
DRINK	Library Bar: drinks, books, games, CDs and DVDs • Pool Bar	
FEATURES	private beach • infinity pool • Mayan-style jacuzzi • steam and dry saunas • thalassotherapy spa • gym • beauty salon • tennis court	
BUSINESS	high-speed Internet access • meeting room • audio-visual equipment	
NEARBY	Pentenpich Bay • Great Mayan Reef • Tulum, Chichén Itzá and Cobá ruins	
CONTACT	Bahía Petenpich km 328, Cancún, Quintana Roo 7750 • telephone: +52.998 872 8300 • facsimile: +52.998 872 8301 • email: resa@paraisodelabonitaresort.com • website: www.paraiso-bonita.intercontinental.com	

Secreto

Traversing the Yucatán area, the Peninsula south of Mexico that has pretty much become the resort playground of the Americas, you might be convinced that huge yachts, a glamorous social scene, beautiful people and fancy speedboats are very much the way of life here.

Come to Isla Mujeres, just a hop from Cancún, and stay at Secreto, and you'll soon understand why the fussiest travellers choose to come to this part of the world to relax. Here, tranquillity rules, leaving the rugged beauty of the island untouched, breathtaking coral reefs undisturbed, and miles of sugar-white sand free for your enjoyment.

Honest, unpretentious authenticity is Isla Mujeres' most precious commodity, and Secreto fits right into the character of the place with hospitality that's elegant, unobtrusive and quietly luxurious. Tucked away secretively (thus its name) in a secluded cove, the discreet three-storey hotel is made even more private through its thick curtain of palm trees that hide it from view.

Rooms are simply but romantically dressed in white and Mediterranean-style wood fittings, including a modern four-post bed with muslin veils. But the star attraction of each room is the scenery—unobstructed with floor-to-ceiling windows. The turquoise

THIS PAGE (CLOCKWISE FROM TOP):
Enjoy cocktails and the sea breeze from your patio; Secreto combines striking architecture with Mediterranean sensuality; every room is designed to exude style and comfort.
OPPOSITE: Original paintings by Mexican artists add colour and drama to the pool deck.

Honest, unpretentious authenticity is Isla Mujeres' most precious commodity...

of the Caribbean Sea seems almost within reach and the salty breeze of the tropical evening envelopes the room.

Privacy is prized at Secreto. Breakfast is delivered to your room, while lunch and dinner are served at the hotel by Rolandi's Restaurant nearby. As the founders of diving expeditions on Isla Mujeres, the owners have built Secreto as a tribute to the island

they love and designed it such that nothing can potentially distract from the appreciation of the beautiful isle. The architecture is modern and unfussy. The pool is surrounded by tropical plants native to the island. And loud discos on the beach, almost an obligatory feature of all resorts on the Yucatán, are blatantly missing here, as are 'social zones' for guests to mingle.

At Secreto, you are encouraged to immerse yourself in marine life. The hotel's dive centre, which organises snorkelling and diving trips, is a good place to begin. Or you could rent a kayak, swim with dolphins or visit the ruins of a pirate's hacienda nearby. Here, you'll finally have a chance to re-acquaint yourself with the Caribbean's beauty, and find a spot to really relax.

FACTS

ROOMS	3 double rooms • 6 king-size rooms
FOOD	nearby Rolandi's Restaurant: wood-fired food
FEATURES	private beach and boat • pool • dive centre • golf carts and bicycles for hire
BUSINESS	meeting rooms
NEARBY	golf course • turtle farm • Cave of the Sleeping Sharks (dive site) • Isla Contoy • Chichén Itzá, Cobá and Tulum ruins • Xcaret and Xel-há ecological parks • Garrafón Underwater Park
CONTACT	Sección Rocas, Lote 11, Punta Norte, Isla Mujeres, Quintana Roo 77400 • telephone: +52.998 877 1039 • facsimile: +52.998 877 1048 • email: reserv@hotelsecreto.com • website: www.hotelsecreto.com

PHOTOGRAPHS COURTESY OF SECRETO.

Shangri-La Caribe

When you are faced with the natural splendours of the Riviera Maya, there's nothing you need more than a hammock under a tree as you allow the soft breeze, gentle heat and the sound of the rolling tide lull you into a sun-soaked stupor. And there's no better place in the world to do this than at Shangri-La Caribe, where civilisation is blissfully worlds away.

A 107-room hotel located in the outskirts of Playa del Carmen, Shangri-La Caribe allows guests to fulfil their island fantasies with a uniquely laid-back approach. Step out of your Mayan-style pavilion with its thatched roof and you'll be treading on silky, white sand. And just a few steps ahead, you'll be greeted with the lapping waves of the Caribbean.

In keeping with the relaxed atmosphere, rooms are located in a nest of Polynesian-style

cabanas, not unlike a fishing village, each no taller than three stories, and offering unbeatable views and access to the sea. Privately owned and operated for over 20 years, the resort is a fusion of warm hospitality and mystic charm, providing for an authentic Mayan-village experience.

Evoking a simple style without the frills, modern trappings such as televisions and in-room telephones are deliberately kept away. The rooms, however, are far from minimalist. Well-lit paths lead you to three different styles of living abodes—Playa, Caribe and Pueblito—all tastefully finished with traditional Mexican furniture, colourful Mexican tiles and woodwork. All rooms come with a patio for those on the ground floor, or a terrace on the upper levels, complete with two hanging hammocks. Indoors, a ceiling fan circulates the breeze.

Though most guests would prefer splashing in the sea or basking on the 820-ft (250-m) stretch of beach, the hotel does offer two large pools and a jacuzzi for those

...the resort is a fusion of warm hospitality and mystic charm...

who prefer some poolside action. There are also daily yoga classes held in an open-air palapa and medicinal plant classes. Or you could try your hand at painting pottery.

And to rid yourself of urban stress, opt for a Temazcal steam bath, said to purify both the body and mind. Filled with such laid-back activities, days meld together blissfully at Shangri-La Caribe.

Meals here are equally relaxed affairs. Treat yourself to a tropical fruit buffet at Aventura, grab a teatime snack by the pool at the Terrace Grill, or wind down to tamales and tostadas at La Loma for dinner. Hardly a deserted island experience, but while you're enjoying your drink with sand on your feet, you'll soon forget the presence of such luxurious conveniences.

THIS PAGE: A lazy afternoon on the private terrace overlooking the endless ocean.

OPPOSITE (CLOCKWISE FROM TOP): Cabanas with coloured walls and indigenous woodwork complete the village landscape; an oasis of sea and jungle surrounds the resort; picturesque views of sand and surf inspire a peaceful stay.

PHOTOGRAPHS COURTESY OF SHANGRI-LA CARIBE.

FACTS

ROOMS	107 cabanas
FOOD	Aventura: breakfast buffet • Terrace Grill: Mexican and international • La Loma: Mexican and international set dinners
DRINK	La Casa Club
FEATURES	2 pools • wading pool • jacuzzi • Temazcal • game room • dive shop • gift shop
BUSINESS	conference room • Internet access
NEARBY	coral reefs • cenotes • Playa del Carmen • Tulum, Cobá and Chichén Itzá ruins
CONTACT	Calle 38 Norte con Zona Federal Maritima, Playa del Carmen, Quintana Roo 77710 • telephone: +52.984 873 0591 • facsimile: +52.984 873 0500 • email: info@shangrilacaribe.net • website: www.shangrilacaribe.net

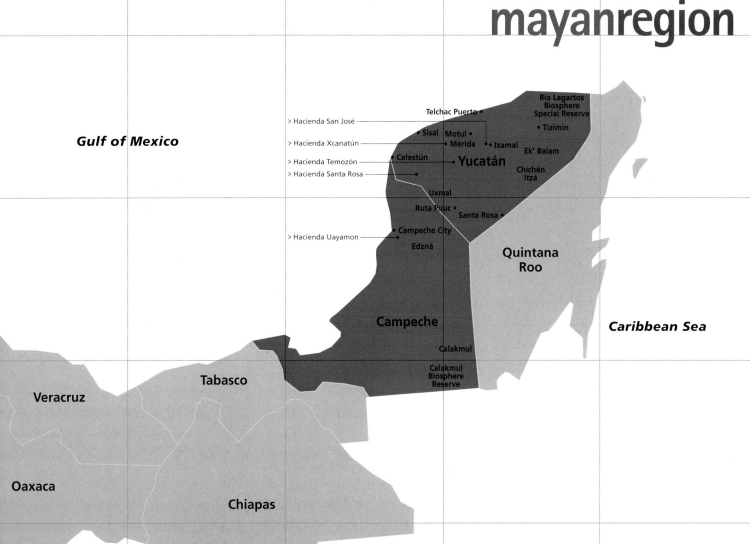

mayanregion

Gulf of Mexico

Caribbean Sea

> Hacienda San José
> Hacienda Xcanatún
> Hacienda Temozón
> Hacienda Santa Rosa
> Hacienda Uayamon

Telchac Puerto
Ría Lagartos Biosphere Special Reserve
Sisal
Motul
Tizimin
Mérida
Izamal
Ek' Balam
Celestún
Yucatán
Chichén Itzá
Uxmal
Ruta Puuc
Santa Rosa
Campeche City
Quintana Roo
Edzná
Campeche
Calakmul
Calakmul Biosphere Reserve
Tabasco
Veracruz
Oaxaca
Chiapas

yucatán: state versus peninsula

Because they share the same name, it is easy to confuse Yucatán (pronounced as 'yoo-cat-AN'), the state, with the Peninsula, which includes the states of Quintana Roo and Campeche, as well as Belize and a small part of Guatemala.

Found in the southeast of Mexico, the Yucatán Peninsula—a low 70,000-sq-mile (181,300-sq-km) tableland—separates the Caribbean Sea from the Gulf of Mexico. It has an assortment of beaches with deep green, calm and shallow waters in the Gulf, and is one of the finest areas for bird-watching in the country. The weather tends to be hot and dry in the northern part of the Peninsula, where rainfall is light (where Yucatán the state is located), but hot and humid further south.

Yucatán state is shaped like an inverted pyramid and occupies 14,868 sq miles (38,508 sq km) of the Peninsula. The landscape is marked with dishevelled ruins, idyllic fishing villages and towns with crumbling convents and old, rambling haciendas—some of which have been converted into classy hotels.

Its rural terrain, rugged with scrub and sapote wood, and peppered with maguey cactus, includes sparkling beaches, cenotes (sink holes), underground rivers and caves, and wildlife ranging from iguanas and armadillos to brightly coloured Yucatecan turkeys.

Mérida, the capital of Yucatán state, is an elegant colonial city known for its museums, murals, folk dance, handicrafts and restaurants. What is probably the country's most distinctive cuisine can also be found in many Yucatecan kitchens.

As the Maya have inhabited the Peninsula since circa 300 BC, the people here continue to use the Maya language, thus adding authenticity and appeal to the place. Some even refer to the area as 'Mayab', meaning 'Maya homeland'.

Spread over 21,622 sq miles (56,000 sq km) of flat land, and comprising most of the Peninsula's western half, Campeche may be larger than Yucatán state but it remains one of the Peninsula's most underrated states. Its coast on the Gulf was a haunt of nefarious pirates, including the English and the Dutch, from the 17th to the 19th century. Many of the old fortifications, bastions, cannons and walled defences that once guarded the port can still be found in Campeche city today.

PAGE 64: The Puuc-style stonework and sculptural details of the Uxmal ruins in Yucatán state.

THIS PAGE (FROM TOP): The handmade embroidered huipil is still worn by the Maya today; a colourful horse-drawn carriage on the streets of Mérida.

OPPOSITE: Flags strung along a colonial church mark Independence Day.

The cobblestone roads of its historic centre are easily explored on foot...

Still a major port, this time-weathered capital is a World Heritage Site. The cobblestone roads of its historic centre are easily explored on foot, with notable sites being the Baluarte de la Soledad (Fortress of Solitude), the city's largest fort; Casa Seis, a restored colonial home that is now a cultural centre; and Yucatan's oldest cathedral, which houses the Nuestra Señora de la Purísima Concepción (Our Lady of the Purest Conception).

For an assortment of quality handicrafts, including embroidered dresses, jewellery, wicker baskets, guayabera shirts and hammocks, Casa de Artesanía Tukulná (House of Crafts Tukulná), is the place to go. The most popular souvenir is the elegant guayabera, a loose, lightweight shirt worn by the Yucatecan upper classes. Most men, and some women, fall in love with this epitome of cool, white tropical wear.

While shopping in town, be sure to drop by any of the restaurants that specialise in mouth-watering Campechan cuisine, such as La Pigua and Restaurant Marganzo, situated just half a block south from Parque Principal, Campeche's main plaza.

The Mayan ruins of Edzná are located 34 miles (55 km) southeast of the city. Much further south, you will find the Calakmul Biosphere Reserve, which is Mexico's largest. At the heart of it lies the remains of Calakmul city, surrounded by dense rainforest, discovered only in 1931. Just 20 miles (32 km) from the border with Guatemala, this archaeological zone covers an area of 44 sq miles (114 sq km) and contains more than 6,000 structures. The few structures already excavated seem to suggest that Calakmul was the largest Mayan city of its time.

The Mayan Express-Yucatán Railway offers an alternative means to visit the ruins. This luxury train ride connects Mérida with Campeche and the intimate jungle ruins of Palenque in Chiapas state, south of Campeche. The interiors of its nine air-conditioned carriages, including those of the cafeteria and dining car, have been hand-painted by Yucatecan artists, and the furniture made by local artisans.

The impressive single-track railway line, built over a century ago, passes through thriving rural communities and Mayan villages, as well as thick jungle, arable farmland and cattle ranches. A full trip takes about two days and includes a visit to Uxmal, and an overnight stay in Campeche city.

THIS PAGE: Stained-glass church window depicting a Franciscan monk deep in prayer.
OPPOSITE: Monument of the Americas in Mérida.

ancient cities

The best-known archaeological sites in the state of Yucatán are the majestic Mayan cities of Chichén Itzá and Uxmal. However, there is also a cluster of overgrown, unexcavated ruins that hold a deep thrill for the adventurous.

The Puuc (Hill) region south of Mérida has more archaeological sites per square mile than anywhere else in the northern hemisphere. The ruins of Chichén Itzá (Mouth of the Well of the Itzáes), are only 75 miles (120 km) east of the city. Visitors are encouraged to go early to beat the crowds and midday sun, which turns the site into a furnace.

Uxmal (Thrice Built; pronounced as 'oosh-mahl') was the greatest metropolitan and religious centre in the Puuc hills between the 7th and 10th centuries. A World Heritage Site consisting of low horizontal palaces set around courtyards and sculptural decorations, this is probably the best-restored and maintained ruin in the Yucatán Peninsula.

At 100 ft (30 m), the tallest structure in Uxmal is the Casa del Adivino (House of the Magician), with its western stairway facing the setting sun at summer solstice. The five-acre (two-hectare) Palacio del Gobernador (Governor's Palace), with sculptures of the rain god Chaac, serpents and astrological symbols, as well as outstanding examples of stone mosaic work, is a wonder. Uxmal also has a large, well-preserved ball court.

A less visited but equally intriguing site is Ek' Balam (Black Jaguar). You have to drive for miles through jungle to get to this treasure trove. Restoration only began in 1997 after archaeologists started digging into the hills covered with trees and bush, and discovered ancient artefacts that had been buried for centuries. The colossal, six-level Acropolis pyramid is the highlight here, and you can climb to the top for a view of the site's other structures, many of which are still awaiting excavation.

hacienda history

Part of an economic system begun by the Spaniards in the 16th century, Mexico's haciendas were large estates that operated in a similar way to America's southern plantations. Haciendas in the Yucatán were built originally for cattle and corn production, but from the 1830s for about a century, they were used for the cultivation and processing of henequen (sisal) to make rope for the booming shipping industry.

The state's haciendas maintained huge fields of henequen, tended by hundreds of Mayan labourers. The largest building was La Casa Principal (The Main House), where business was administered and where the hacendado (landowner) resided. Henequen processing took place in La Casa de Máquinas (The Machine House), and some of the original machinery used for processing the fibres can still be seen at a handful of remaining haciendas. There would also be a capilla (chapel), a house for the foreman, storage buildings and smaller living quarters for the workers on each property.

When demand for oro verde (green gold, as henequen was nicknamed) was at its highest, there were around 1,000 henequen haciendas. However, the industry collapsed with the invention of synthetic fibres and most of the region's haciendas were abandoned in the 1940s. The rise of these haciendas overlapped with one of the most dramatic events in Mexican history—the revolt of the Maya of Yucatán against their white and mestizo rulers known as La Guerra de Las Castas (The Caste War). Considered by modern historians to be the only successful native-American rebellion,

this uprising began in 1847 and ended in 1855, killing or putting to flight almost half the population. Even today, Yucatán's upper classes prefer not to speak of the atrocities.

In the 19th century, Fernando Carvajal, owner of Hacienda Uayamón and one of the great

THIS PAGE (FROM TOP): The rustic blue façade of Hacienda San José; a stone sculpture of Chaac, the god of rain, in the ruins of Chichén Itzá.

OPPOSITE: During excavations, archaeologists uncovered treasures hidden behind these Ek' Balam structures.

entrepreneurs of his time, built the local Campechan steam railway. His concern for the health and education of his workers also led to the introduction of electricity.

Abandoned to the elements, the haciendas were swallowed up by jungles until the 1990s, when a wave of investments led to the restoration of buildings and land for homes, museums, restaurants and luxury hotels. The isolation and romantic pasts of these haciendas proved very attractive for travellers looking for a place that was stylish, private, full of character and completely out of the ordinary. Being part of a conservation effort, they also had plenty of ecological appeal.

As 'hacienda fever' developed, greater care was taken to preserve their original building materials and ambience. Hacienda Xcanatún, which opened as a hotel in 2002, is the result of massive reconstruction and careful restoration of the original space and ornamentation of the buildings, using only local materials such as hardwood, wrought iron, clay, glass, marble and coral stone. This conservation project took eight years to complete.

There are five haciendas in Mérida, and 25 listed in the state—some still in working condition, others in crumbling ruins, and a few laid out as museums. Hacienda Santa Rosa offers a particularly interesting bicycle tour around the abandoned haciendas. In the northeast of Mérida, Hacienda San José is the most secluded of the Yucatán haciendas and offers tours to Motul, a typical Mayan village.

But there is nothing quite like living in one for a taste of the affluent lifestyle enjoyed by the lords of the region. In Hacienda Temozón, for example, much of the original décor, including the red and yellow mineral pigments used to colour the stucco walls, and the exquisite floor tiles that were imported from Italy aboard the returning henequen boats, has been preserved.

THIS PAGE: *The majestic Hacienda Temozón with its spectacular pool and plush interior.*

OPPOSITE (FROM TOP): *In the 19ᵗʰ century, henequen (sisal) was cultivated to produce rope; the ubiquitous hammock is a prominent feature in haciendas.*

white city

When the Spaniards arrived, Mérida was a large Mayan city known as T'hó, situated on what is now known as Plaza Mayor, the city's main square. Conquistador Francisco de Montejo the Younger founded this lime-mortared colonial city in 1542, naming it after the Roman ruins of Mérida in Extremadura, Spain.

Soon after, all the pyramids were dismantled and their huge stones were used as foundation for Catedral de San Idelfonso, the oldest cathedral on the American continent. Directly across the square from the cathedral is the Palacio Municipal, Mérida's Town Hall, while on the south side is Casa de Montejo, the conqueror's former home. Another site of interest is the town hall, Palacio de Gobierno (Government Palace) on the north side, which houses 27 vivid murals by Fernando Castro Pacheco, illustrating the violent history of the Conquest.

Now, with over a million inhabitants, Mérida is one of Mexico's leading cultural hubs. Every Saturday, restaurants bring out their tables so guests can linger over a late Yucatecan lunch on the pavements and watch life go by. The city's graceful architecture lined with laurel trees is a delight, and its fine museums deepen any understanding of Yucatán's inimitable character.

The museums to visit are the Museo de Antropología e Historia (Museum of Anthropology and History) in the Palacio Cantón, dedicated to the culture and history of the Maya, and the Museo de Arte Contemporáneo Ateneo de Yucatán (Museum of Contemporary Art).

The main square, Plaza Mayor, referred to as the zócalo elsewhere in the country, is also called El Centro, Plaza Principal or Plaza de la Independencia by the Meridanos. Take a walk or a calesa (horse-drawn carriage) down the 19th-century boulevard, Paseo de Montejo, from which Mérida got its name and see the gleaming white stone of the stately mansions and homes here.

On Calle 47 (Street 47), a free spectacle of regional music performances, folkloric dance and handicrafts for sale are showcased

THIS PAGE (FROM TOP): *Whitewashed mansions line the sidewalks of Paseo de Montejo; Hacienda Santa Rosa's chapel.*
OPPOSITE (FROM TOP): *Catedral de San Idelfonso houses Mérida's most revered statue of Christ, El Cristo de las Ampollas; the horse-drawn calesa is a great way to get around and take in the sights.*

on Noche Mexicana (Mexican Night) every Saturday. The Mercado Municipal Lucas de Gálvez, Mérida's main market, and Casa de las Artesanías, a market for local artisans, are also places to visit for craftwork. The latter sells anything from wicker baskets and figurines of deities to earthenware and wind chimes.

Locally made Panama hats woven from palm leaves can also be found here, though the Campechan town of Becál is the centre of the hat trade. Organised tours in Mérida often include private visits to artisans' studios, a workshop where Panama hats are made, musical performances and cigar shops.

With the sweltering heat accompanied by humidity, you will find many local people sleeping on hammocks, strung from wall hooks or outside between trees. Walk down any street in Mérida and you'll see hammocks hanging in the balconies of hotels and homes.

Izamal is known as La Ciudad Amarilla (The Yellow City) for its old houses painted in egg-yolk yellow and white.

The best Yucatecan hammocks are made here—the heart of the hammock industry—and they are sold on almost every street corner. Their fine strings are woven from cotton or nylon, which makes them extremely comfortable. Dyed in different colours, they are also available in various sizes and standards of durability. For quality hammocks, stick to reputable hammock stores, instead of buying them from peddlers on the streets.

Among the cultural highlights in Mérida are the Ballet Folklórico which performs most Friday nights at the Universidad Autónoma de Yucatán (Autonomous University of Yucatán), while the municipal cultural centre, Olimpo, is a hub for events.

yellow city

To experience provincial life, the magical city of Izamal—known as La Ciudad Amarilla (The Yellow City) for its old houses painted in egg-yolk yellow and white—and the traditional Mayan town of Tizimín are the places to visit.

Probably the oldest city in the state, Izamal was founded by a Mayan patriarch in the fourth century and is one of the jewels of the Peninsula. It is also called the City of Hills as it was built on an archaeological site, and the town centre is distinctively humpy with pyramids, including the enormous 115-ft (35-m) Kinich-Kakmó. Transformed into an important Christian sanctuary by the Franciscans, it has a rich history that you can absorb while bobbing along cobblestone streets in a calesa.

The main attraction in Izamal is the Franciscan monastery, Convento de San Antonio de Padua (Convent of San Antonio de Padua). It has the largest atrium in Mexico, and the church houses a statue of Our Lady of Izamal, Yucatán's patron saint. The antics of the monastery's founder, Fra Diego de Landa, make for a poignant tale: he burned all the Indian scripts documenting Mayan history and habits, then struck by guilt and remorse, attempted to rewrite everything based on memory.

In the northeastern part of Yucatán, 100 miles (161 m) east of Mérida, Tizimín is a picturesque city that is still rich in tradition. Also known as the City of Kings for its 17th-century temple, Parroquia Los Santos Reyes de Tizimín (Church of the Three Wise Kings), it is not frequented by tourists and hence offers authentic insights into a real Mayan town.

THIS PAGE: *The blazing sun makes hats a necessary part of everyday attire.*
OPPOSITE: *The unmistakable yellow archways of Convento de San Antonio de Padua in Izamal.*

taste tango

Yucatán is often referred to as 'la tierra del faisan y el venado' (the land of the pheasant and the deer), and has a gastronomic tradition of unique ingredients and flavours.

Complementing the ubiquitous sopa de lima is the signature dish, cochinita pibil. This classic recipe consists of pork marinated in achiote, sour orange juice, peppercorns, garlic, cumin and salt, then wrapped in banana leaves and baked. It is usually served with maize tortillas and salsa habanera, made from the hot habanero chilli, on the side. Those who prefer chicken will find an alternative in pollo pibil.

Other traditional main courses are relleno negro (turkey with stuffing), usually prepared with minced beef, charred chilli sauce, and queso relleno (stuffed cheese), a European-inspired creation consisting of a whole Edam cheese which has been hollowed out and stuffed with a type of spiced ground meat called picadillo.

Poc chuc—tender slices of pork marinated in sour orange juice, cooked over a wood-charcoal fire, and served with pickled onions—is an interesting dish for palates that are drawn to tangy tastes. A local delicacy is the unusual papadzul (or papatz tzul), a soft taco containing boiled egg drenched in a creamy pumpkin seed sauce, which can be eaten as a main course or snack.

If you are likely to be one of those who wake up craving for a hearty Mexican breakfast, Motul-style eggs often served with fried slices of plátano macho (plantain), is the speciality of Yucatán. This is a robust meal of tortilla (handmade with maize rather than cornflour) covered with refried beans and a fried egg, then drenched in tomato sauce and accompanied by peas, chopped ham and shredded cheese.

Appetisers such as panuchos, salbutes, tamales, empanadas and garnachas are great for kick-starting a meal. The most distinctive of these are the panuchos, made from fried tortilla dough, and served with refried beans, shredded chicken, lettuce strips, diced onion and salbutes, prepared in a different shape with the same ingredients, minus the beans. Other regional highlights include chirmole, a flavouring paste made of dry-roasted chillies, and pipián, a stew similar to the mole usually containing zucchini seeds and nuts.

The Peninsula is also renowned for its seafood. Coastal towns such as Telchac Puerto or Celestún offer an idyllic combination of relaxing beaches and a mouth-watering mix of fresh ceviche, lobster, tuna, marlin, conch and octopus. Campechan cuisine also has a niche of its own, with favourites being seafood dishes such as camarones al cocado or al mango (shrimp with coconut or mango), and different preparations of cazon (baby shark).

wet sites

As in Quintana Roo, cenotes (sinkholes) are one of the more unusual natural wonders of Yucatán state. One of the best places for a guided cenote tour is Cuzama, where you can travel through the countryside in a horse-drawn cart to visit the cenotes of Chelentun, Chansinic'che and Bolonchoojol. Cenotillo is another village where, according to locals, there are over 150 cenotes. Some of these are found in open fields.

The Loltun caves—whose name comes from Lol (flower) and Tun (stone)—are the largest in the Peninsula. Mammoth bones and wall paintings have been found here. Even closer to Mérida, the Tzabnah Caves include 13 cenotes, and a huge chamber known as the Cúpula del Catedral (Cathedral Dome).

Filled with stalactites and stalagmites, the limestone Balankanche caves were an important ceremonial site used by the Maya to make offerings to the rain god. One of the caverns features an enormous, pillar-like stalagmite in the middle that reaches to the ceiling, with Mayan ceremonial objects arranged around it. The site includes a small museum and a light-and-sound show.

The flamingos are another attraction of the area. The largest flocks of these peculiar, salmon-pink birds in North America can be found in the wetlands of the Yucatán, especially Ría Lagartos, northeast of Mérida and Celestún, an ecological sanctuary in Campeche. The best time of year to visit is between March and August, and the best time of day is at sunrise or sunset. Take a boat trip through the thick mangroves or swim in a cenote. A guide will point out some of the 99 species of water birds in residence.

THIS PAGE (FROM TOP): Fresh fruit and vegetables sold on the streets; the largest colony of flamingos in North America can be found in the wetlands of the Yucatán.

OPPOSITE (FROM TOP): The distinct flavours of Yucatecan food have made it synonymous with Mexican cuisine; a family-run food stall in Mérida.

Ría Lagartos is part of a Biosphere Special Reserve near the state's border with Quintana Roo, where bird watchers can also spot cormorants, great white herons, snowy and red egrets, peregrine falcons and white ibis. The estuary encompasses a 'petrified forest', where trees that once belonged to a freshwater ecosystem are now infused with saltwater, keeping them tough as rock and towering high.

Those who wish to indulge in as much sea life as possible can visit the Arrecife Los Alacranes (Scorpion Reef; named after its shape) and its surrounding five islands. Here, you can scuba dive to see rainbow-coloured fish and also look out for some 250 shipwrecks lurking in these waters.

maya modern

It is in the state of Yucatán where the Peninsula's Mayan culture and language are best conserved as the Maya have inhabited the region for over 2,600 years. Visitors with an aptitude for linguistics will soon recognise the style and inflections of this ancient tongue in the names of the places, people and regional dishes.

Besides the language, elements of Mayan religion and cosmology are still part of the living culture. While they have fallen prey to modernisation, it is interesting to note that they have preserved many of their rites and rituals, dances and costumes. The influence of Mayan art can also be found in the paintings, clothing, weavings, textiles, masks, silver jewellery, sculptures and the famous Yucatecan hammocks.

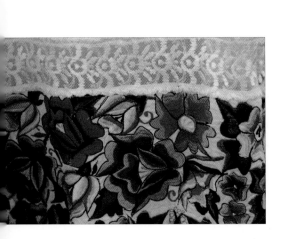

Typical dwellings are oval-shaped thatched huts, while clothing is mostly white with coloured embroidery on the women's blouses. The Museo del Pueblo Maya in the Dzibilchaltun ruins exhibits Mayan artefacts, such as the symbolic huipil (indigenous-style blouse), from all over Yucatán. On your way back from Uxmal, you can stop at the village of Villa de Santa Elena and visit local Mayan families who will explain the use of herbal medicine and demonstrate the cooking of tortillas over an open fire in their homes.

It used to be difficult to entice tourists from the idyllic Caribbean beaches to the historic treasures of this area. But as awareness of its rich history, culture and heritage increases, discerning travellers are returning again and again to the Yucatán.

THIS PAGE: Many of the Maya still live in traditional thatched huts as their ancestors did, keeping their culture alive.

OPPOSITE (FROM TOP): The finest and most expensive hammocks are hand-woven from silk; much labour goes into creating the intricate embroidery typical of the Yucatán.

Hacienda San José

For visitors to Mexico, haciendas conjure up surreal images of colonial plantations. With unsurpassable grandeur, they dominated lush plantations with ranches, chapels, manicured parks and fountains. But no matter how wild one's imagination may be, it's impossible to really comprehend the magnitude of major haciendas during the centuries of colonial rule. Some were as large as Belgium and the dominant ones had become elaborate institutions with stables, a general store, a school, granaries and a forge.

The prosperous haciendas were often host to celebrations: saints' days, fiestas, bullfights and harvest festivals. Scenes at these affluent homes were usually raucous, with much dancing, drinking and feasting.

Then came the revolution of the early 20th century that finished off many of the

THIS PAGE (CLOCKWISE FROM TOP): *Large and luxurious suites are perfect for relaxing after a trip to the Mayan ruins; the hotel's massive pool is designed to impress; private pools and gardens may be found in some suites.*

OPPOSITE: *Regional specialities can be enjoyed outdoors on the terrace or in the gardens.*

haciendas. Most were burnt and pillaged, and left in ruins with nothing but a few basic walls. Today, the few remaining haciendas are regarded as gems of Mexico's history. Those that have been discovered have been beautifully restored and transformed into country homes or luxury hotels.

Especially prized are the haciendas in the Yucatán Peninsula. The centre of the sisal boom in the 19th century, many were owned by sisal lords and barons and were opulently decorated with exquisite imported European materials. One of the more outstanding remaining haciendas in that region is Hacienda San José, located in the quiet town of Tixkokob, north of the Yucatán Peninsula. It was the home of a 19th-century nobleman who created a neoclassical building that was in keeping with the architectural trend then.

Hacienda San José has since been turned into an exclusive boutique hotel with just 15 rooms. Despite its grand halls and soaring ceilings, the hacienda is infinitely warm and welcoming. The façade has been painted in soothing turquoise while the rooms are washed in cheerful citrus shades. Some suites open out to private gardens, terraces and swimming pools, although the main pool on the grounds more than suffices for a refreshing swim.

Though still relatively unknown, being one of the more discreet haciendas in the area, the hotel is popular with discerning honeymooners and couples who are intrigued by the chapel on its property.

Hacienda San José also offers all the modern conveniences guests would expect of a five-star property, despite retaining the colonial spirit of the place. These, of course, have never before been a part of a traditional hacienda. Certainly there's no better time to experience the lavish lifestyle of a hacienda owner than now.

FACTS

ROOMS	11 rooms and suites • 4 Mayan villas
FOOD	San José restaurant: regional
DRINK	San José lounge and bar
FEATURES	19th-century hacienda • private pools and gardens in some suites • chapel manicured gardens • pool
BUSINESS	meeting and event facilities
NEARBY	Izamal city • Telchac Puerto • Mérida city • Progreso Port • Chichén Itzá ruins
CONTACT	Carrertera Tixkokob-Tekanto km 30, Tixkokob, Yucatán 97470 • telephone: +52.999 910 4617 • facsimile: +52.999 923 7963 • email: reservations1@grupoplan.com • website: www.starwood.com

Hacienda Santa Rosa

Hacienda Santa Rosa stands out as the most charming example of an intimate boutique hotel, where a visit is rather like staying with friends, with cosy rooms and a warm, sincere welcome. Very exclusive with only 11 rooms, it enjoys a relaxed ambience and leisurely pace. Peacocks strut about in manicured gardens and the smell of fresh flowers perfumes every room.

Though situated just 32 miles (52 km) away from Mérida city, Hacienda Santa Rosa seems worlds apart from modern urban life. It is situated at the edge of a rustic Mexican village where fishermen still ply their boats, and the hotel's architecture and design capture poignantly the colonial grace of a bygone era. Much of the original structure—arched verandahs, high-beamed ceilings, enormous wooden doors and cool floor tiles—has been retained. Adding character to the décor are antique furnishings and vibrant hues of deep red, sky blue and ochre on the walls.

Each of the 11 rooms is luxuriously decked with antique iron bedsteads and hand-embroidered bed linen. Spacious with high ceilings, some of them have private terraces, garden areas and large bathrooms as well as private pools for some suites. The Mayan Villa, a self-contained bungalow with a plush king-size bed suspended by ropes and covered with plump white cushions, is designed for die-hard romantics.

In the evenings, 'friends' of the hacienda can look forward to converging

THIS PAGE (FROM TOP): Occupying an original 18th-century building, the hotel offers guests the grand lifestyle of sisal barons; each suite mirrors the luxurious details that come with a nobleman's private estate.

OPPOSITE: Rooms are fronted by private patios and pools.

for meals at Hacienda Santa Rosa's terrace which overlooks the pretty fruit-filled garden. They may also choose to dine in one of the grand reception rooms or enjoy an intimate, candle-lit dinner anywhere they wish in the hotel.

The menu features a selection of Yucatecan specialities, with pastas and salads available throughout the day. Guests can also drive out to Celestún, a small fishing village in the middle of a bird sanctuary for freshly-caught seafood. Another highlight of Hacienda Santa Rosa is its bar. Ironically, it was formerly a quaint chapel on the hacienda's grounds with original tiled flooring and period furniture.

The hacienda is ideally located in the heart of the Mayan archaeological zone. In its vicinity are numerous sights of historical significance. They make tearing yourself away from the beautiful Hacienda Santa Rosa almost worth it.

FACTS		
	ROOMS	10 rooms • 1 Mayan villa
	FOOD	dining room: Yucatecan specialities, pastas and salads
	DRINK	lounge bar
	FEATURES	flower and fruit gardens • pool • private pools in some suites • private terraces in all rooms
	BUSINESS	meeting and event facilities
	NEARBY	Uxmal ruins • Mérida city • Celestún fishing village • Oxkintok • Calcehtok caves
	CONTACT	Carrertera Mérida km 129, Campeche, Santa Rosa, Yucatán 97800 • telephone: +52.999 910 4852 • facsimile: +52.999 923 7963 • email: reservations1@grupoplan.com • website: www.starwood.com

PHOTOGRAPHS COURTESY OF STARWOOD HOTELS AND RESORTS, AND HACIENDA SANTA ROSA.

Hacienda Temozón

If stepping into Hacienda Temozón feels like coming home, it's probably because it was once the majestic residence of one of the most influential sisal lords of the 19th century. Certainly the grandest restored hacienda in the Yucatán Peninsula, Hacienda Temozón awes with long corridors, lofty halls, soaring ceilings, sweeping verandas and lawns of greenery.

With the faithful replication of its original décor, Hacienda Temozón still retains the splendour of the colonial era. The property is so meticulously preserved that almost all the elaborate Italian tiles decorating the hallways are still intact. Even the original reddish pigment used to colour the walls remains vibrant.

Situated just outside the city of Mérida on a former henequen plantation that extends 1,359 acres (550 hectares), the hotel is now open to guests wishing for a true hacienda experience. Twenty-eight rooms in the main building are welcoming and luxurious with brass or wooden beds furnished with hand-embroidered linen and lace. Many have separate living areas and some even feature private plunge pools that are discretely shielded with dense foliage.

Hacienda Temozón may first impress with its unsurpassable grandeur, but residing guests will soon appreciate the other more homely aspects of the hotel. Hammocks are offered in all rooms for lounging, and unexpected passageways lead to secret gardens and cosy niches. And should guests wish for a soothing massage, a wide range of in-room services, including authentic Mayan treatments, are available.

And then there's the location—idyllic and secluded in the heart of the Mayan countryside, and yet just 24 miles (39 km) away from the nearest airport and town. Guests seeking to immerse themselves in the rich cultural heritage of the Yucatán Peninsula will also find it an excellent starting point to many of the important Mayan ruins, such as the dazzling Puuc sites of Uxmal and Kabah. In fact, there is so much to explore that guests usually have a hard time choosing between ultimate relaxation at the hacienda or fascinating excursions in the neighbouring area.

Returning after a day-long adventure at the sites, guests can expect a warm welcome with gourmet Mexican specialities which they may enjoy wherever they choose: on the second-floor restaurant overlooking the grand pool and gardens, in their rooms, or on the outdoor terraces. Though Hacienda Temozón may be the ideal gateway to Mayan culture and history, it's also an indulgence for those seeking sheer luxury.

THIS PAGE (CLOCKWISE FROM BELOW): The spectacular 157-ft (48-m) pool with a swim-up bar; rooms feature the design traditions of a 19th-century hacienda, but are outfitted with the latest communication tools.

OPPOSITE (FROM TOP): The hacienda's sprawling grounds include a 17th-century church; the restaurant offers a heady mix of Mexican and creative transethnic fare.

FACTS

ROOMS	28 rooms
FOOD	Temozón Restaurant: local and eclectic
DRINK	Bar Temozón
FEATURES	pool • tennis court • 91-acre (37-hectare) garden • private pools in some rooms
BUSINESS	meeting rooms • event facilities
NEARBY	Mérida city • Uxmal and Kabah ruins • Loltun Caves • Progreso Port
CONTACT	Carretera Mérida-Uxmal km 182, Temozón Sur, Yucatán 97825 • telephone: +52.999 923 8089 • facsimile: +52.999 923 7963 • email: temozon@grupoplan.com • website: www.starwood.com

Hacienda Xcanatún

Surely one of the most palatable ways of acquainting yourself with the local culture is to taste it. In Yucatán, you won't find a better guide to Mayan culture than at Casa de Piedra, an award-winning restaurant set in the intimate Hacienda Xcanatún (Tall Stone House) boutique hotel. Here, you'll have a sampling of authentic Yucatán ingredients—habanero chilli, achiote seed, loganza (sausage) and sour orange—fused with Caribbean flair and French finesse. Certainly, the sumptuous spread at Casa de Piedra recalls the time of the traditional

haciendas, owned by rich landlords who feasted on the finest meals everyday.

Like the cuisine it serves, the hotel is equally rich in Mayan culture and history. To relive the lavish style of the landlords, you might want to book into the 18-suite Hacienda Xcanatún, an 18th-century estate, whose colourful history includes being owned by a famous local family before becoming one of the most important producers of sisal (agave plant) in the area. But like all good things, this period too ended and Hacienda Xcanatún was

THIS PAGE (CLOCKWISE FROM TOP):
A classic hacienda comes alive with an elegant blend of ochre-coloured walls and coral stone; a water reservoir has been transformed into one of two pools that are sustained by subterranean rivers; suites are decorated with antiques, colonial-style furniture and Peruvian oil paintings.
OPPOSITE: A full-service spa employs traditional Mayan healing techniques to detoxify and rehydrate the body.

relegated to becoming a summer home, only to be abandoned shortly after.

But the hacienda lives once more under the hands of Cristina and Jorge Ruz, who had visions of converting the noble ruins into a luxurious establishment. After five years of intense reconstruction, Hacienda Xcanatún entered the 21st century with a new and glamorous identity, and is now a member of Mexico Boutique Hotels.

Through the talents of the local architects and craftsmen, Hacienda Xcanatún now surpasses its original beauty and preserves its cultural heritage, while providing guests with all the indulgences of a modern hotel. It even scooped an AAA Four Diamond Award and the Five Star Diamond Award from The American Academy of Hospitality Sciences.

The building's history may be recognised through its architecture. The chapel has become the hotel's lounge; the machine room for sisal production is now home to the restaurant, reception and four new suites with colonial furnishings, polished stone floors and handcrafted stone sculptures.

Two freshwater pools, lush tropical gardens and a full-service spa complete the compound. Equipped with five treatment rooms and separate steam baths, the spa offers deep tissue massages, reflexology, aromatherapy and facials treatments as well as holistic Mayan treatments.

The final result is a blend of the historic and the contemporary, combined with the personalised service of the only privately owned and managed hacienda hotel in Yucatán. Located minutes away from Mèrida city, Yucatán's capital, and the pyramids and temples of Chichén Itzá and Uxmal, Hacienda Xcanatún is a wonderful starting point to discover the identity and culture of the place. But don't forget to make Casa de Piedra restaurant your first stop.

FACTS

ROOMS	18 suites
FOOD	Casa de Piedra Restaurant and Bar: international, local and Caribbean
DRINK	Casa de Piedra bar
FEATURES	spa • 2 pools
BUSINESS	meeting facilities
NEARBY	Chichén Itzá and Uxmal ruins • wildlife refuge • cenotes • Mérida city
CONTACT	Mérida-Progreso Highway km 12, Xcanatún, Mérida, Yucatán 97300 • telephone: +52.999 941 0213 • facsimile: +52.999 941 0319 • email: hacienda@xcanatun.com • website: www.xcanatun.com

Hacienda Uayamón

It has been said that Campeche is Mexico's best-kept secret. A little walled city north of the Yucatán Peninsula, it is pretty with narrow stone streets lined with neoclassical town houses. Particularly striking are those in the old quarter painted in intense shades of yellow, pistachio, pink and robin-egg blue. Its cheerful façade today belies its dramatic history. The fortress surrounding the city is a result of frequent attacks by pirates in the 1500s, and Campeche is the only city in Mexico to be thus protected. Today, visitors can amble through its well-preserved dungeon-like alleyways to be whisked away to that ominous era 500 years ago.

Campeche is also priceless for its archaeological sites, including the famous Edzná, Jaina, Chicanna, Izpihil and Calakmul ruins, that are over a thousand years old. Despite their prominence in Mayan history, they are still relatively tourist-free and secluded, promising an unbeatable exploration experience, like a traveller coming upon a lost civilisation.

Hacienda Uayamón is the perfect place to reside in while you're in Campeche. It melds with the rich history of its surroundings with grounds that date back to 1700. A beautiful example of colonial architecture of that period, it features grand rooms with soaring ceilings, arched doorways and walls painted warm shades of maroon and mustard.

Hacienda Uayamón started life as a wood-dye factory, and in the 19th century, it was converted into a sisal plantation with outhouses for its high-ranking employees. In

THIS PAGE (CLOCKWISE FROM TOP):
The pool is designed to embrace the features of colonial architecture; originally a wood-dye factory, the 18th-century building has been transformed into a chic 12-casita retreat; gourmet meals may be enjoyed almost anywhere in the hotel.

OPPOSITE: Former employee hostels have been restored to luxurious guest suites.

It melds with the rich history of its surroundings with grounds that date back to 1700.

its latest transformation to a luxury hotel, these hostels have been turned into 12 elegant casitas. Though the living quarters are now sumptuous and grand, with rod-iron beds, plush white linen, mahogany furniture, and black-and-white tiles, guests are reminded of Hacienda Uayamón's past by structures that have been deliberately left in ruins. Particularly poignant is the magnificent swimming pool. While guests dip into its cool blue water, the vestiges of an old factory lie crumbling around them.

Located in a quiet part of Campeche, guests can enjoy a peaceful stay in rooms with private gardens edged by a tropical jungle. The hotel transforms into a candle-lit fantasy in the evenings with hundreds of delicate flames lighting the way to each room.

Amid this magical setting, meals are enjoyed on the open grounds of the hotel with a hearty selection of international cuisine. Alternatively, guests could drive out to the nearest town square and listen to jazz at an outdoor café, enjoy a Cuban dinner at one of many fine restaurants, or simply walk the streets with a corn tortilla in hand. At the end of the evening, guests heading back for a tranquil night's rest could look forward to the next day's exploration, or simply an afternoon of sheer relaxation at the hotel.

FACTS

ROOMS	12 casitas
FOOD	Uayamón Restaurant: international
DRINK	Uayamón Bar
FEATURES	18th-century building surrounded by 'ruins' • large gardens • pool
BUSINESS	meeting facilities
NEARBY	Campeche city • Edzná ruins • Jaina Island • Mérida city
CONTACT	Carretera China-Edzná km 20, Uayamón, Campeche • telephone: +52.981 829 7526 • facsimile: +52.999 923 7963 • email: reservations1@grupoplan.com • website: www.starwood.com

PHOTOGRAPHS COURTESY OF STARWOOD HOTELS AND RESORTS, AND HACIENDA UAYAMÓN.

centraleast+southhighlands

Durango

Coahuila

Nuevo León

Zacatecas

Tamaulipas

San Luis Potosi

Aguascalientes

Gulf of Mexico

Jalisco

• San Felipe

• León

Guanajuato

> Quinta Las Acacias —— • Guanajuato City

Querétaro

Hidalgo

Colima

Michoacán

Mexico State

Tlaxcala

Amecameca Volcano • • Iztaccihuatl Volcano

Mexico City   • Popocatépetl Volcano   • Pico de Orizoba Mountain

> Casa Tamayo Cuernavaca ——   Puebla City • • La Malinche Volcano

• Cuernavaca

Cholula •   Orizaba •   > Mesón Sacristía de la Compañia

> Mesón Sacristía de la Capuchinas

Morelos   > El Sueño Hotel + Spa

Puebla   > La Quinta Luna

Tehuacán •

Veracruz

• Teotitlán del Camino

Guerrero

> Camino Real Oaxaca

> Casa Cid de Leon

Oaxaca City •

Oaxaca

San Felipe del Agua • ——> Hacienda los Laureles

Monte Albán •

Pacific Ocean

Mitla •

> Camino Real
Zaashila Huatulco

Bahías de Huatulco •

Puerto Ángel •

model city

The vast city of Oaxaca, with its shady zócalo (town square), 16th-century cathedral, elaborate colonial buildings and mural-adorned government palace, owes its fame to the beauty of its architecture and folk art, and the richness of its cultural traditions and cuisine. Not only is this image intact—the city's green-hued stone and crafts markets, the strolling musicians, food vendors and Triquis women dressed in traditional huipiles can still be seen—it is also becoming more polished.

Oaxaca (pronounced as 'wah-hah-kah') is carefully maintained through cultural and social development projects, making it Mexico's model city for poise, heritage and local pride. Cobblestone streets sprinkled with immaculately preserved buildings such as the gothic Church of Santo Domingo—with its ornately-carved baroque façade, white and gold leaves, bell towers and intricate paintings—have been the result.

The city is known for its fine handicrafts, along with its museums, art galleries and lively dining, nightlife and music scenes. Its large and highly artistic indigenous population is the driving force behind the booming arts industry and worldwide demand for Oaxacan crafts. Some of the art to look out for include the alebrijes (fantasy creatures made of wood), black pottery, hand-woven rugs, textiles and tapestries. Traditional crafts aside, it is also the capital of contemporary Mexican art, attracting artists, art dealers and buyers from far and wide.

Cosmopolitan touches abound but on every corner you will still find townsfolk peddling their wares, dotting the streetscape with anything from colourful costumes and shoeshine stands to stalls selling fruit, gardenias and chapulines (fried grasshoppers). Life is centred around the traffic-free zócalo and the adjacent Alameda Plaza, where everyone gathers during the day, making it perfect for watching the crowd go by. At night, mariachi bands play under colonial archways or in the wrought-iron bandstand.

Nearby, located within a 25-mile (40-km) radius of the city, the archaeological ruins of Monte Albán, Mitla and Yagul built by the Zapotec and Mixtec people, testify to their ancient cultures. The majority of Oaxaca's residents are descendants of these indigenous tribes that flourished in the area thousands of years ago. Monte Albán contains over

PAGE 92: *The Cathedral of Tlaxcala, 19 miles (30 km) north of Puebla.*

THIS PAGE (FROM TOP): *A column-lined courtyard leads to the Museo de las Culturas of Oaxaca which displays relics from Tomb 7 at Monte Albán; the gilded interior and altar of Oaxaca's most lavish church, Iglesia de Santo Domingo.*

OPPOSITE: *The church of Nuestra Señora de los Remedios sits upon the Great Pyramid of Cholula, overlooking the Popocatépetl volcano.*

200 lavish tombs and 300 burial sites, while Mitla's ruins are unique for their abstract geometric patterns and brilliance of stone. The palace ruins of Yagul—a fortress-like city standing atop a hill above a group of palaces, temples and underground tombs—aren't nearly as complicated, but still worth a visit.

A population of about 800,000 is sprawled across the high, fertile plateau of Oaxaca Valley filled with deep caverns and virgin beaches, and encircled by the majestic Sierra Madre del Sur mountain range. Thanks to its high elevation, the city enjoys a sunny, spring-like climate all year round with cool evenings and warm days, and the hottest months being April and May.

city of angels

Lying 60 miles (96 km) southeast of Mexico City is the City of Angels—Puebla. Few Mexican cities uphold the Spanish imprint as faithfully as Puebla, as it was built from scratch by the Spanish colonists who arrived in the New World with the intention of settling, rather than returning to Spain after the Conquest.

With more than 70 churches, chapels and ex-convents, Puebla retains a strong religious and conservative air. The town's cathedral, whose steeples stand among the highest in the country, is a prominent landmark that blends Herreresque-Renaissance and early baroque styles, as does the Ex-Convento de Santa Rosa, which now houses a collection of religious and folk art.

Hand-painted tiles known as Talavera (named after a town in Spain) enliven the splendid 17th-century façades of the historic centre with their bold colours. You'll see these tiles adorning the homes, churches, patios, fountains and government buildings all around. Talavera in the form of plates, cups, vases and other crockery can be found at the El Parián crafts market and the open-air antique market of Plazuela de los Sapos.

As it is also a centre for education, Puebla brims with university students and has a youthful atmosphere and bustling nightlife. Long-haired youngsters strum guitars as townsfolk lay out handicrafts on the pavement to sell. It has some of Mexico's most memorable museums and thousands of valuable books housed in the ancient

THIS PAGE (FROM TOP): Puebla's colonial architecture is sharply contrasted with modern, bright colours; Talavera tiles are a striking example of Pueblan exuberance, artistry and workmanship.
OPPOSITE: A typical Spanish-style building with a tiled façade and wrought-iron balconies.

Few Mexican cities uphold the Spanish imprint as faithfully as Puebla...

THIS PAGE (FROM LEFT): *The dome-shaped bell tower of Oaxaca's cathedral blends geometric patterns with Arabic design; the townsfolk of Oaxaca.*

OPPOSITE (FROM TOP): *Remnants of a colonial structure in Veracruz; traditional carriage.*

Biblioteca Palafoxiana (Palafox Library). In the evenings, live music fills the air from the cafés and bars of Puebla and nearby Cholula.

These two eponymous city states lie east and southeast of Mexico City: Puebla is accessible under two hours by road, and Oaxaca, a little under five. It is one of the most exciting highways out of the capital, full of promise and adventure, leading to the smoky volcano of Popocatépetl and its silent northern neighbour, Iztaccíhuatl, Mexico's second- and third-highest mountains respectively. The imposing Popocatépetl has enjoyed intermittent periods of activity for centuries (the most recent in 1994), adding a further apocalyptic edge to this triumphant descent on the Valley of Mexico.

Visitors to Puebla often hike up the dormant volcano of La Malinche, about 15 miles (25 km) northeast of Puebla, whose enormous jagged crater and sweeping slopes cut across the skyline. Past Puebla, near the turn-off south towards Tehuacán Valley and Oaxaca, you will see the country's highest peak, the snow-capped Pico de Orizaba which stands at 18,405 ft (5,610 m). Its steep cone fills the sky of Orizaba town, which lies at the mountain's base.

Amecameca is also worth a stop on the way to Puebla. With its two volcanoes as a backdrop for the town's activities, it makes a captivating walk with fantastic views of the peaks and the village sprawled out beneath them. With the help of a guide, you can try climbing Izta's highest peak, El Pecho, which requires an overnight stay on the mountain. But if you prefer to enjoy the scenery from a safe distance, El Paso de Cortés has a freshwater trout farm nearby where you can fish and dine beneath the pines.

Head straight eastwards and you will reach the festive city of Veracruz, the Spaniards' most important port and gate of entry into Mexico. In the early 16th century, Cortés marched his men from here—picking up disgruntled warriors for his army on the way to fight the Aztecs—between Popocatépetl and Iztaccíhuatl. Today it is famous for its frenetic celebration of Carnival, also known as Mardi Gras, which stands as Mexico's biggest and wildest revelry, where bands play infectious rhythms and street performers dressed in colourful costumes parade the streets in song and dance.

mole mecca

Puebla may have made its mark on Mexico's culture, but it is also celebrated for its flavourful cuisine, often imitated throughout the country. It is here that mole poblana, or spicy (not sweet as most people would expect) chocolate-based sauce, served over turkey or chicken, was invented. It can be found on almost every menu in Puebla.

A long-established culinary delicacy, mole has gradually travelled out of the region in the last decade. It is famed for being the most complicated Mexican savoury sauce that has up to 40 ingredients, which often includes fresh chilli, chipotle (smoke jalapeño), cinnamon, peanuts, sesame seeds and dark bitter chocolate.

There are several variations of this heady sauce and many towns that claim to be the birthplace of mole (pronounced as 'mo-lay'), but in Puebla, you can put an end to this mystery. Here you can visit the kitchen of the Ex-Convento de Santa Rosa, where the nuns supposedly invented mole, and even hear an explanation for its name. The kitchen has a beautiful workshop decorated with exquisite tiles and big-bellied clay and copper pots, while the centre displays regional ceramics and a museum shop.

Mole poblana contains the tasty chilli poblana, a thinner and darker version of the green bell pepper. Almost bland before it is cooked, it may be served in rajas (strips), a side dish in which it is fried with a little onion and cream, or as a filling for tortillas. It is also used in soups that are often referred to as campesina (countryside), with fresh mushrooms (a delicacy in the rainy season), zucchini flowers and elote (corn).

As you will observe in Oaxaca, mole comes in different colours—green, brown, black, red and yellow. A red Oaxacan mole has the notorious reputation of being a 'mancha manteles' (tablecloth stainer). Some are nutty or sweet, while others taste of pumpkin seed, as do many green moles. Red moles are great with pork, and yellow ones have a strong almond flavour that complements fish.

Visitors looking to bring a taste of Puebla home can buy mole in the market as a powder or paste. Both forms transport well, although it is best to buy it as a paste, sealed tightly in a jar. You can then add chicken broth to it or anything else you fancy when cooking at home, and serve it with meat, fish or rice.

THIS PAGE (FROM TOP): *Tropical fruit is in abundance in the marketplace; restaurant signboard; mole powder, maize grains and spices for sale.*
OPPOSITE: *Restaurants in Oaxaca offer a wide range of regional and international cuisines.*

Puebla is also the birthplace of Mexico's national dish, chiles en nogada...

Puebla is also the birthplace of Mexico's national dish, chiles en nogada (stuffed poblano peppers in walnut sauce), usually served during Independence Day celebrations or on special occasions. A seasonal dish available mainly in September, it is intimately connected with Mexico's fiestas patrias (patriotic festivities).

Large green chillies are stuffed with shredded pork, raisins, white walnut cream and red pomegranate seeds. The dish, whose cheery colours of red, white and green are those of the Mexican flag, is sweet and sometimes a little spicy depending on how hot the chillies are. It is a delicacy with layers of complex flavours that are skilfully balanced and can be quite costly as the sauce has to be made with fresh walnuts.

Another treat to look out for in Puebla are chalupas—corn tortillas shaped like small boats and fried until crisp. They are usually filled with shredded meat, vegetables or cheese (or a combination of all) and served as an appetiser.

When in Oaxaca, be sure to try the Mexican rendition of the pizza—tlayuda, a giant grilled tortilla smeared with fried beans, green chilli, avocado, shredded cheese and the meat of your choice.

lavish tombs, hidden treasures

The best way to explore the states of Puebla and Oaxaca is to wander around on foot, where you will find yourself weaving in and out of a mesh of indigenous cultures. Even in cosmopolitan Oaxaca city, the streets are filled with women carrying baskets on their heads, wearing traditional huipiles (embroidered blouses) and skirts, walking barefoot and selling their wares.

Oaxaca is the home of the Zapotecs and Mixtecs, who form a majority of the 15 indigenous groups in the state, followed by the Mazatecs, and other groups including the Mixes and Triquis. Zapotec and Mixtec cultures reached significant heights in Oaxaca's three central valleys before the arrival of the Aztecs in the 15th century. The population of the Zapotecs peaked between 300 and 700 AD, with about 30,000 inhabitants centred around the great pyramids of Monte Albán, 6 miles (10 km) west from Oaxaca city. The Mixtecs later took over the Zapotecs' holy city as a burial site and built lavish tombs which have since been uncovered to reveal over 500 priceless treasures including gold breastplates, jade, pearl and ivory.

Spilling over 28 miles (46 km) southeast of Oaxaca, Mitla was also a Zapotec settlement and a religious centre, where human sacrifices were performed by high priests. Its name means 'place of the dead' and unlike other ruins, there are no human figures or mythological events represented—only abstract designs, which make this site striking. Mitla was eventually taken over by the Mixtecs who began to dominate around the 12th century.

For an unusual introduction to Puebla's pyramids, head for the widest pyramid ever built—El Gran Pirámide de Cholula or the Great Pyramid of Cholula. It has been tunnelled through at a disorientating angle, so you can trawl through the base of this seven-storey pyramid to the temple of Nuestra Señora de los Remedios. Claustrophobes should opt instead for a gentle hike to the recently renovated Santa María de los Remedios Church that the Spaniards built atop the ancient structure, which affords a regal view of the volcanoes.

shop stops

Puebla and Oaxaca have a long history of artistic traditions, not only in handicrafts but also in the fine arts, such as engraving and photography. Shopping is top-notch in both states—Puebla is popular for antiques, onyx and ceramics, while Oaxaca is sought after for its pottery, hand-woven products and alebrijes.

In Puebla, El Parián Market is best for ceramics shopping, as is the Uriarte Talavera, which has a ceramics workshop where you can see the process of ceramic making on guided tours. For the sweet-toothed, Calle de las Dulces (Street of Sweets) is the place for fruit-flavoured candy, while huipiles (embroidered blouses) and any type of indigenous clothing can be bought in Cuetzalan, the northern part of Puebla state.

THIS PAGE (FROM TOP): The elegant spine and dome of a church in Cuetzalan, Puebla; embroidered sombreros.

OPPOSITE (FROM TOP): Classical columns support an unexpected skylight formed by ruins; the charm of Oaxaca lies in its friendly people; the ancient Zapotec capital of Monte Albán.

The colonial town of Cuetzalan is famed for its Sunday market that attracts scores of indigenous people dressed in traditional costumes, filling the zócalo on weekends. Here, four hours from Puebla city, most of the population are women—usually barefoot, however chilly the climate, carrying wares for sale on their backs.

In Mitla, alebrijes, or brightly coloured mythical creatures carved from copal wood, will cost a third of the price of those sold in the city. They make great gifts as toys—Oaxacan artisans have been carving them for their children for centuries. While in the area, you can also bargain for shawls.

On the road to Mitla (along highway 190), the shops at the charming weaving village of Teotitlán del Valle provide demonstrations on how natural dyes are made from dried insects and native plants. Rugs, wall hangings, satchels and other woven goods are also sold here.

cousin mescal

Central Oaxaca state produces the best mescal in the world and there's no better place to shop for mescal than in the villages between the south and east of Mitla. Clusters of street stalls sell mescal in decorative bottles, indicating that this is the liquor of choice. Like its cousin tequila, mescal is made from the maguey plant and tastes better when aged. It is known outside of Mexico as 'the drink with a worm in it'.

In the city and in almost any town around, you can find it on sale everywhere, often with a dash of red salt made from powdered gusano (worm). An inexpensive and extremely potent drink, some claim that it can cause hallucinations. Unlike tequila which has a finer flavour, mescal is an acquired taste with its smoky undercurrents and rougher edge.

The worm, which is really a maggot or larva, is there to indicate the drink's high alcohol content as it keeps the worm from rotting. Consuming the worm from a bottle of mescal is part of urban legend, but worm-eating itself is not—the maguey larva is eaten, but as a delicacy, fried and usually served with guacamole in a warm tortilla.

party nation

It is important to know when the fiestas fall in this part of Mexico, not only because it is worth visiting when a party is going on, but also because if you wish to be part of these immensely popular celebrations, you will need to book your accommodation well in advance, or risk missing out on the festivities.

On May 5, there is a parade in Puebla city to celebrate Cinco de Mayo, which is not just a one-day national public holiday, but an entire month of fiestas held throughout Puebla state with bullfights, dance performances, musical concerts, food festivals, sculpture workshops for children, and so much more.

The patron saint of Oaxaca, Mexico's fifth-largest state, is the Virgin of Solitude, and December 18 is the day to honour her—be it in Oaxaca city or anywhere else in the state. In Puerto Escondido for instance, the church's image of the virgin is brought to land on a rowboat heralded by waterborne trumpets at sunset.

The Guelaguetza is Oaxaca's massive regional dance festival that lasts over a week in the second half of July, uniting the different regions of Oaxaca in traditional dress, dance, music and movement. It is Mexico's most extravagant dance show and tickets should be booked by March the latest. Thousands of locals and tourists flock to the outdoor Auditorio Guelaguetza on Cerro del Fortin hill to partake in this rhythmic celebration of regional culture.

Day of the Dead is a favourite festival in Oaxaca. It represents an unusual blend of Catholic and indigenous traditions, and is both a celebration of the living and the dead. During this time, the city and all its surrounding villages come alive with flowers, food, glowing candles, decorated graves and folklore. A bizarre display known as the Noche de los Rábanos (Night of the Radishes) draws the crowds,

as radishes are shaped into nativity scenes and displayed in the zócalo for a prestigious competition in the run-up to Christmas.

Carnival, and in particular Shrove Tuesday, is a highlight of the communities living around the Popocatépetl volcano, especially in Amecameca, east of Mexico City, and Huejotzingo in Puebla state. The fair of San Francisco is celebrated by the town of Cuetzalan in early October, while Christmas sees a beautiful nativity display of mammoth proportions in Puebla city's Amparo Museum.

royal retreat

The City of Eternal Spring, Cuernavaca lives up to its reputation with gloriously inviting climate and abundance of exotic foliage, as well as an attractive colonial town centre. The capital of the state of Morelos, it is also within easy reach of ancient ruins, hot mineral springs, old haciendas and mansions too numerous to count.

Cuernavaca was the country escape of Emperor Moctezuma who kept his botanical gardens here. Hernán Cortés' medieval-style fortress also stands here at the end of Plaza de Armas, Cuernavaca's zócalo. Today, the city remains a magnet for the wealthy and powerful, and a retreat from Mexico City as it did in colonial times when conquerors, rulers and aristocrats were attracted to its rural settings.

Although there is plenty to see and do—from the grand Palacio de Cortés (Cortés' fortress) with murals by Diego Rivera and the Robert Brady Museum, to the 18th-century Baroque-style Recinto de la Catedral, and the elegant Jardín Borda (the summer residence of Emperor Maximilian and Empress Carlota from 1866)—much of the town's sophistication is kept hidden behind its high walls. Opulent banquets, royal weddings and other high-brow events are reserved strictly for Mexico's elite.

Just over an hour away from Mexico City, Cuernavaca is a delightful place for a day visit. Its charming restaurants, museums and galleries, the Salto de San Antón waterfall and gardens festooned with peacocks and flowering herbs, continue to make this little town a modern-day paradise.

THIS PAGE (FROM TOP): The tradition of the village brass band is still very much alive in Oaxaca; once-grand portals lead to a churchyard in Morelos.
OPPOSITE: The fortress-like Palacio de Cortés (Palace of Cortés) stands in the centre of Cuernavaca.

Camino Real Oaxaca

After visiting Mexico City and the Mexican Riviera, where sprawling hotels and beach raves are very much part of the scene now, you wonder if it is possible to experience the mystery, beauty and history of the country's rural charm, without having to share it with busloads of tourists.

The answer is 'yes' if you know where to look. If you wish to enjoy Mexico in its most authentic and unadulterated state, head for Oaxaca, which is relatively untouched by colonialism and tourism, and where 14 native ethnic groups still flourish.

The magic, culture and customs of the Zapotecs, Mixtecs and other tribes continue to dominate much of everyday life in Oaxaca, where the people are still ruled by rites and traditions. Festivals are a weekly occurrence here, and vividly hued costumes can be spotted among the womenfolk.

Complementing the Old World charm of Oaxaca is Camino Real Oaxaca—a much cherished 16th-century landmark of the area that was formerly the Convent of Santa Catalina. The history of the hotel mirrors that of Oaxaca, starting with the arrival of the Dominicans in 1528. The convent was established to assist in the mission of evangelism in the area, but was converted into a prison 200 years later.

It was not until the 1970s that the property was recognised as an architectural gem and extensively repaired. Original frescoes (16th-century wall paintings), a legacy of the building's first inhabitants, were rediscovered and the elaborate flooring restored to its former glory, along with the graceful archways, ornate fountains, patios and courtyards. The quaint and informal Camino Real Oaxaca opened in 1994 with 91 suites, each looking out to delicately scented jasmine gardens, grand courtyards or picturesque street scenes. The polished wooden beams, mosaic floors, tapestries and locally handcrafted fabrics that furnish the rooms are a reminder of the building's history, combined with 21st-century hospitality and comforts.

THIS PAGE (FROM ABOVE): The hotel is dotted with charming courtyards and ornate fountains; one of Mexico's most cherished landmarks, this beautifully restored hotel was once a convent.

OPPOSITE: Guests can retreat to the pool for a dip or enjoy cocktails on the terrace.

Camino Real Oaxaca is also an ideal place to sample Oaxaca's distinctive cuisine—considered the most varied and complicated in Mexico. At El Refectorio, you can taste the spicy, chocolate-based mole sauce, a Mexican speciality that requires at least 31 ingredients. There are also Las Bugambilias in the courtyard and Las Novicias by the pool to enjoy an aperitif, cocktail or nightcap while admiring the 'singing' fountain, gardens and details of an era so splendidly preserved here.

Guests can also look forward to the traditional celebration of 'La Guelaguetza', held weekly at the hotel's hall, which was formerly the convent's chapel. Here, you can enjoy a fiesta of ethnic dances and costumes from seven regions, an Oaxacan buffet and a merry market of local artefacts and wares. It is an experience that is not only out of this world, but also completely out of this time.

FACTS

ROOMS	51 deluxe suites • 34 Camino Real Club suites • 6 junior suites
FOOD	El Refectorio: Oaxacan and international
DRINKS	Las Novicias poolside bar • Las Bugambilias courtyard bar
FEATURES	pool • satellite television • scented gardens • theme parties
BUSINESS	4 meeting rooms • Los Lavaderos and Los Naranjos patios for outdoor events
NEARBY	museums • art galleries • cafés • artisan markets • Santo Domingo Cathedral • Macedonio Alcalá theatre • Monte Albán and Mitla ruins
CONTACT	Calle 5 de Mayo 300, Oaxaca 68000 • telephone: + 52.951 501 6100 • facsimile: +52.951 516 0732 • email: oax@caminoreal.com • website: www.caminoreal.com/oaxaca

Camino Real Zaashila Huatulco

THIS PAGE (FROM ABOVE): A striking white façade complements the cloudless blue skies of Huatulco; the modern resort resides in a former fishing village.

OPPOSITE: Guests enjoy the option of lounging in their private plunge pools or swimming laps in the spectacular main pool.

One look at the lobby of Camino Real Zaashila and you'll have an idea what the weather is like in Huatulco, Mexico. There are no doors and it is exposed to the elements throughout the year. Of course, guests at the 120-room resort by Tangolunda Bay wouldn't be expecting anything less than cloudless skies, balmy breezes and perennial sunshine. After all, it's been said that the climate at Huatulco is so blissful even Acapulco would be envious.

Newly discovered as a beach town just 10 years back, Huatulco was formerly a fishing village with plans of being transformed into the next Los Cabos. Blessed with the best natural amenities—powdery beaches, clear blue waters and rugged scenic mountains—it is predicted Huatulco will be transformed into a booming seaside resort by 2020 when plans to develop all of the area's nine bays are complete.

But till then, there's time to enjoy paradise till the crowds come: all 22 miles (35 km) of picture-perfect beaches along a nearly virgin Pacific coastline graced with nine crystal sparkling bays. Huatulco, which lies in the state of Oaxaca, enjoys magnificent views due to its stunning location, where the foothills of the Sierra Madre meet the waves of Mexico's Pacific Ocean. It is an amazing, exotic and mysterious coast of secret coves and hidden lagoons.

One of the first hotels in Tangolunda Bay, Camino Real Zaashila is situated on

a wide stretch of private sandy beach and secluded from other beaches by small rock outcroppings. Here, the water is calm, clean and blue—perfect for swimming and snorkelling.

The hotel is by no means small, but buildings are low rise and well separated to ensure privacy. Rooms are generously large and luxuriously appointed with ocean-view balconies and terraces, marble tubs and wicker finishing. Camino Real Club rooms also feature pretty plunge pools, but with the fabulous 328 ft (100 m) meandering pool just steps away, you'll find it hard to decide where to soak.

Unlike other luxury hotels in Mexico, Camino Real Zaashila is actually child-friendly. The spacious one- and two-bedroom suites are ideal for travelling families, and there are well-planned children's activities as well as childcare amenities available.

And while the kids are baking in the sun, parents can have a peaceful meal at any of the three restaurants on the premises: Club de Playa, the casual joint by the ocean front that serves up seafood; Bel La Grill, the breakfast buffet outlet; and the chic Chez Binni, that specialises in traditional Oaxacan fare.

There's also Bitza Lounge Bar for tropical cocktails. This is the ideal place to contemplate what to do next: take a boat out to visit the other eight pristine bays, hit a couple of balls on the lush Tangolunda Golf Course, or just sit back and relax, knowing that you're among the first few to discover paradise.

FACTS	
ROOMS	79 deluxe rooms • 41 Camino Real Club rooms
FOOD	Chez Binni: Oaxacan • Club de Playa: seafood • Bel La Grill: breakfast buffet
DRINK	Bitza Lounge Bar • Bar Bel La Grill: drinks and snacks by the pool
FEATURES	private beach • 2 pools • outdoor jacuzzi • fitness centre • Miss Chief Club for children • private plunge pools in Camino Real Club rooms
NEARBY	Tangolunda Golf Course • 8 other bays and beaches • shops at La Crucecita village • Parque Botazoo nature reserve
CONTACT	Boulevard Benito Juárez 5, Bahía de Tangolunda, Bahía de Huatulco, Oaxaca 70989 • telephone: +52.958 581 0460 • facsimile: +52.958 581 0461 • email: zaa@caminoreal.com • website: www.caminoreal.com/zaashila

Casa Cid de León

THIS PAGE (CLOCKWISE FROM RIGHT):
Every element in the Bella Época suite—from embroidered linen and crystal lamps to fresh bouquets of flowers—suggests luxury and hospitality; detail of a stone mantel with cherub in the Aranjuez suite; a spiral staircase flanked by religious wall art, leads to the rooftop garden terrace.

OPPOSITE: *Dinner for two in the Dominica Suite is a popular choice for honeymooners.*

Oaxaca is one of those magical destinations that blend history and culture with a healthy dose of folklore. Walking through the city's cobblestone streets, passing the historic zócalo (town square), and observing the harmonious interaction of Oaxaca's 27 ethnic groups is an exciting experience in itself. And then there are the weekly street festivals or fiestas—colourful celebrations of food, dance, costumes and music—that shouldn't be missed.

Oaxaca is mysterious and exotic, yet incredibly vibrant. It is altogether an enchanting destination. And Casa Cid de León is a charming boutique hotel in the area that is in keeping with the quaintness of the town and offers the most intimate form of hospitality. Formerly a small colonial house, it has been converted into an exquisite hotel that is surely the most exclusive with only four large suites.

...'Casa Cid de León is not just a hotel. It is also a mirror of our guests' personalities.'

Previously the home of the Cid de León family, the three-storey residence has been exquisitely restored in extravagant 18th-century European style with a touch of Mexican cheerfulness. Delicate floral chintz, bronze chandeliers and ornamental angels in the suites are eclectically featured against terra cotta floors, exposed ceiling beams and green limestone.

Each suite is furnished to reflect its individual character and name. The Belle Época suite is a popular choice among honeymooners seeking a romantic experience. It is intimate and feminine with apple-green walls, floral upholstery, a grand bathroom and three balconies. Travelling families can stay in the Mio Cid suite, formerly the Cid de León sons' rooms which are spread across two floors and have direct access to the garden terrace.

The hotel suites are individually decorated so that guests may pick the

theme that most appeals to them. The owners see themselves as hosts, taking great pride in the grandness of their home and the comfort of their guests who are made to feel like they too, own the hotel. According to them, 'Casa Cid de León is not just a hotel. It is also a mirror of our guests' personalities.'

On the third floor, guests relax and mingle on the rooftop terrace that serves as the dining room, lounge and bar, where delicious family recipes and botanas (Mexican snacks) are specially prepared by the owner, Augustine.

Best of all, Casa Cid de León is ideally situated in the heart of downtown Oaxaca, where guests may spend the day exploring the city on foot. Within walking distance are the cathedral, Santo Domingo Cultural Centre, Rufino Tamayo and contemporary art museums, Macedonio Alcala Theatre and Soledad Temple. And in the evenings, they can head back to Casa Cid de León—a magical home away from home.

FACTS

ROOMS	4 suites
FOOD	terrace garden: family recipes and botanas (Mexican snacks)
DRINK	bar at the terrace garden
FEATURES	jacuzzi in 3 suites • 2 bathrooms in Mio Cid suite • satellite television
BUSINESS	private office or children's room (functions as work area) in each suite • Internet access
NEARBY	cathedral • Santo Domingo Cultural Centre • Macedonio Alcala Theatre • Rufino Tamayo and contemporary art museums • Soledad Temple
CONTACT	Avenida Morelos 602, Centro Histórico, Oaxaca 68000 • telephone: +52.951 514 1893 • facsimile: +52.951 514 7013 • email: reservaciones@casaciddeleon.com • website: www.casaciddeleon.com

PHOTOGRAPHS COURTESY OF CASA CID DE LEÓN.

Hacienda los Laureles

At the edge of the rustic village of San Felipe del Agua, Hacienda los Laureles, with its sculptured gardens and magnificent laurel trees, embodies every romantic vision you would expect of a retreat. There are wide and long verandas lined with colonial columns, high ceilings, arched windows and stately wooden furnishings that are typical of traditional haciendas. Just 10 minutes from the zócalo of Oaxaca city, but

without the traffic and noise, this boutique hotel is similar to the luxurious inns characteristic of the historic town. But the hotel offers the unbeatable advantage of space—great expanse of tranquil gardens for guests to walk or jog through. The surrounding mountains, ecological reserve and great outdoors beckon, allowing guests to make the most of the area's glorious summers and mild winters.

...the hotel comfortably toes the line between luxury and homeliness.

The hacienda is the fulfilment of a dream by owners Peter Kaiser and his wife Ligia—both experienced hotel administrators who had been searching for a suitable place to create their own ideal nook in the fringes of the city. They explored the land of Mexico for three years, and finally chanced upon an old hacienda in this small and charming village.

Rebuilt from the ground with new water pipes, drainage systems and electrical cabling, Hacienda los Laureles was certainly not easy to create. Today, it is a five-star hotel with 23 rooms, a swimming pool with a jacuzzi, a fitness centre, a spa and a gourmet restaurant specialising in elaborate Oaxacan cuisine.

In keeping with the provincial feel of the village, yet catering to the many international guests it receives, the hotel comfortably toes the line between luxury and homeliness. Chintz fabrics are draped on elegant wrought-iron beds, while colourful Mexican carpets add an air of informality to European rooms. And everywhere you look, there are beautiful tapestries, magnificent porches and refined millwork framing the rooms.

A recent addition to the property is Petit Spa, a sanctuary seriously dedicated to wellness. It offers massages, facials, body treatments, reflexology, aromatherapy and Temazcal—an indigenous steam bath for detoxifying the body. All this, of course, is best combined with an afternoon stroll through the beautiful San Felipe mountains, or a round of tai chi, yoga or reiki in the peaceful hotel gardens.

With its emphasis on luxury, warmth, comfort, rich food and complete serenity, Hacienda los Laureles is the ultimate retreat in the country. Guests will find it impossible not to be charmed by an experience of such grand Mexican style.

FACTS		
ROOMS	8 deluxe rooms • 8 superior rooms • 3 master suites • 4 junior suites	
FOOD	Los Cipreses: Oaxacan, Mexican and international	
DRINK	Los Cipreses	
FEATURES	heated pool • jacuzzi • fitness centre • spa • Temazcal	
BUSINESS	business centre • 2 meeting rooms • audio-visual equipment	
NEARBY	golf course • Monte Albán, Yagul and Mitla ruins • Benito Juarez National Park	
CONTACT	Hidalgo 21, San Felipe del Agua, Oaxaca 68020 • telephone: +52.951 501 5300 • facsimile: +52.951 501 5301 • email: bookings@hotelhaciendaloslaureles.com or inquiry@hotelhaciendaloslaureles.com • website: www.hotelhaciendaloslaureles.com or www. hotelhaciendaloslaureles-spa.com	

El Sueño Hotel + Spa

If you are thinking of taking a tour through Mexico, be prepared to pack a large suitcase as there is a different ensemble for every destination. Along the coast facing the sunny Caribbean, lycra swimwear is the order of the day. Travel inwards and you'll need to pile on the sweaters.

The climate here is astounding as it is quite possible to experience all four seasons in a day. What's relatively unknown, however, is the pleasant perpetual spring of the country's middle highland plateau. At 7,000 ft (2,134 m), the height spares the land from the otherwise sultry weather. As a result, more visitors to the country are discovering the delights of visiting central Mexico, especially in the mountain towns that cluster around Mexico City.

One of the places worth visiting is Puebla, a quintessential Mexican city with beautiful baroque-style architecture. Home to many mansions, convents and churches, the buildings here are far grander than any other colonial city, with the heavy use of painted tiles, gold leaves and moulded plaster.

Another outstanding feature of the town is its cuisine, which has contributed much to Mexican gastronomy. The country's celebrated mole poblano, a mixture of chilli sauce and chocolate, was created by the

THIS PAGE (CLOCKWISE FROM ABOVE): The Patio de San Miguel is one of three courtyards guests can retreat to for outdoor drinks; a modern remake of an ancient mansion, the hotel's interior is as welcoming as its façade.

OPPOSITE (FROM LEFT): Racy crimson walls and elements of wood and steel add a contemporary edge; the sky-lit courtyard is the perfect spot for afternoon tea and lounging.

While its façade retains its pompous grandeur...the interiors are surprisingly modern...

nuns at the Convent of Santa Rosa in Puebla. The origins of tinga (pork or chicken stew) and mixotes (meat wrapped in a tamale and steamed) have also been traced to this town.

Best of all, the city that continues to burgeon with commercial and industrial activity, offers all kinds of accommodation for the visitor. One of them is El Sueño Hotel and Spa, an exclusive 11-suite hotel that has been converted from an 18th-century baroque residence. While its façade retains its pompous grandeur with columns and arches, the interiors are surprisingly modern with sleek fittings of aluminium and glass. Dedicated to 11 internationally famous women including Mexican painter Frida Kahlo, rooms offer views of the magnificent Cathedral Angelopolitana.

Leisurely days can be spent combing the stall-lined streets for antique treasures, or indulging in a relaxing massage at the hotel's spa. Besides the treatment rooms, the spa also offers a jacuzzi, steam room, pressure shower, outdoor solarium and gymnasium.

Meals are savoured outdoors on the patio where the best of Pueblan cuisine is presented, while the indoor lounge serves gourmet snacks all day. Guests can enjoy a selection of courtyards, where running water from the antique stone sinks soothes and placates. The only catch is the absence of a beach, but after a few days at El Sueño Hotel and Spa, guests will most certainly realise they don't need one.

FACTS		
	ROOMS	11 suites
	FOOD	lounge: cakes, savouries and gourmet snacks
	DRINK	café • lounge
	FEATURES	spa • gym • jacuzzi • steam room • outdoor solarium • pressure shower
	BUSINESS	meeting and event facilities • Internet access
	NEARBY	Cathedral Angelopolitana • Amparo Museum • zócalo (town square) • old Sapos neighbourhood
	CONTACT	9 Oriente 12, Centro Histórico, Puebla city, Puebla 72000 • telephone: +52.222 232 6489 • facsimile: +52.222 232 6423 • email: hfdzdelara@elsueno-hotel.com • website: www.elsueno-hotel.com

PHOTOGRAPHS COURTESY OF EL SUEÑO HOTEL + SPA.

La Quinta Luna

Not too far away from Puebla, amid the fertile fields of maize, lies Cholula, a famed ceremonial town dedicated to the deity Quetzalcotl. Hernán Cortés described it as 'the most beautiful city outside of Spain', and in a bid to colonise it, destroyed its temples and replaced them with many shrines and churches, including the famous 49 domes of the Capilla Real.

The most famous feature of Cholula, however, is the Great Pyramid—the largest ever built, eclipsing even Egypt's grand pyramids of Giza. But because it is so overgrown with vegetation and topped by the church of Nuestra Señora de los Remedios, it's more like a huge grassy mound rather than a pyramid. Within it however, lies the most elaborate maze of tunnels, the result of several temples built over one another over thousands of years. Visitors can now travel through a major tunnel that crosses the entire pyramid, which has been excavated by archaeologists.

The town itself has a quaint provincial feel, and much of the population consists of indigenous people who resolutely retain

THIS PAGE (CLOCKWISE FROM TOP):
A wine-coloured façade is matched with colonial arches, balconies and intricate wrought-iron work; the central courtyard where a magnificent fountain bubbles; amid the soothing palette of cream and camel furnishing are the riotous shades of modern art hanging on the wall.

OPPOSITE (FROM LEFT):
Meals may be enjoyed in a garden surrounding; or in the cosy dining room.

Despite the highly stylised design of the hotel, it remains hospitable and friendly...

many of their own pre-Spanish customs. Plaza squares are colourful arenas of festivities and market activities, while cafés and restaurants line the main streets.

Cholula is also home to one of the most elegant boutique hotels of the Pueblan region—La Quinta Luna, a six-bedroom abode located in the oldest and most historic part of town in Santa Maria Xixitla.

Beautifully preserved, this 17th-century former nobleman's residence presents an exquisite contrast of classic architecture with modern interiors. Even the bathrooms are works of art with intricate mosaic decorations alongside the generously sized baths. The highlight of the hotel, however, must be its old-fashioned library which holds some 3,000 books, and it is built from the dark wood beams excavated during the renovation of the property, which dates back to the 17th century.

Despite the highly stylised design of the hotel, it remains hospitable and friendly, due to the graciousness of its owners, the Cárdenas González de Cossío family, who live on the hotel grounds and serve their guests. Ultimate privacy is guaranteed, with the property more than large enough to accommodate its handful of guests.

In the evenings, La Quinta Luna adopts a more mellow, romantic mood, with candles and dimmed lighting softening its scarlet shade and casting a reddish glow on the grounds. Dinners are best enjoyed on the patio where guests can enjoy the garden scenery. The hotel's restaurant, Antigua Capilla, offers all that La Quinta Luna embodies—a refreshing slice of the modern with all that is authentic and traditionally Mexican.

FACTS

ROOMS	3 standard rooms • 2 master suites • 1 junior suite
FOOD	Antigua Capilla: traditional and modern Mexican, and international
DRINK	bar and lounge
FEATURES	library with over 3,000 books • guided tours upon request
BUSINESS	meeting facilities • Internet access
NEARBY	Great Pyramid • Casa del Caballero Aguila Museum • Puebla city • Tonanzintla • church • Cacaxtla and Xochitécatl ruins • ancient city of Tlaxcala
CONTACT	3 Sur 702, Cholula, Puebla 72760 • telephone: +52.222 247 8915 • facsimile: +52.222 247 8916 • email: reservaciones@laquintaluna.com • website: www.laquintaluna.com

Mesón Sacristía de Capuchinas

In a broad, high valley about 60 miles (97 km) southeast of Mexico City is a city known by many names over the years: City of Angels, City of Tiles and Heroic City of Zaragoza, just to name a few. Today we know it simply as Puebla.

Established by the Spanish in 1531, Puebla was the principal city of colonial Mexico and is considered the most European of all the colonial cities. Its friendly residents, the Poblanos, have a reason for their immense pride in their city. Planned from the ground up by a Spanish city designer rather than being built within an existing Indian community, Puebla, not unlike Paris, is immaculately structured and magnificent in its grandeur.

Shortly after the Spanish conquest, Puebla became well known throughout Mexico for milling, textiles, hand-made pottery and tiles, as well as the architectural beauty of its buildings. Although modern Puebla is highly industrialised, its historic downtown area remains a Spanish-colonial treasure filled with elegant 17th- and 18th-century European architecture and art.

You now have a chance to stay in one of the grandest buildings in Puebla with the opening of Mesón Sacristía de Capuchinas—the second boutique hotel in

THIS PAGE: *Diners can opt for a romantic meal in the hotel's quaint courtyard.*

OPPOSITE (FROM LEFT): *Like the restaurant's design, the cuisine is contemporary-international with a Pueblan flair; each room is individually decorated with a fusion of modern and rustic elements.*

the city established by the famed Espinosa family. Just a couple of minutes walk away from Mesón Sacristía de la Compañía, the original Mesón Sacristía hotel, de Capuchinas adopts a similar theme of a niche antique hotel, with guestrooms and public areas decorated with vintage furnishings collected by the Espinosas who are antique dealers.

But unlike the first hotel, de Capuchinas resides in a far grander property—a 450-year-old building that was formerly the residence of an aristocratic family. In keeping with the scale, de Capuchinas turns away from the homely rustic ambience of la Compañía and is decorated in a stylishly modern mode with a cool palette of white, aquamarine, and citrine. Here, the contemporary feel is dramatically contrasted with the worn edges of time with a display of thoughtfully chosen antique pieces. And as with la Compañía, these may be yours to buy should you take a fancy to them.

Mesón Sacristía de Capuchinas is highly exclusive and only lets seven rooms. Each room is spacious, with a different layout and individually furnished with unique pieces from the family's collection. Despite its foot in the past, the hotel remains relevant to today's guests with a complete range of modern amenities.

The cuisine it offers is as avant-garde as the hotel. In its smart 30-seat restaurant, the food parallels the hotel's sleek and modern edge, serving up contemporary versions of international classics. There are, of course, Pueblan touches in the menu. These however, are given newer, lighter finishes. As with the rest of de Capuchinas, everything is refreshingly stylish and chic, yet in keeping with the historic roots of its locale.

FACTS		
	ROOMS	7 rooms
	FOOD	Restaurant-bar Capuchinas: home-made Mexican
	DRINK	Capuchinas bar
	FEATURES	Historical 450-year-old building with modern design and antique furnishings
	NEARBY	Plazuela de los Sapos market for Pueblan food and wares • museums • cathedrals • historical buildings • zócalo (town square)
	CONTACT	9 Oriente 16, Antigua Calle de Capuchinas, Centro Histórico, Puebla 72000 • telephone: +1.800.712 4028 or +52.222 246 6084 • facsimile: +52.222 232 8088 • email: sacristia@mesones-sacristia.com • website: www.mesones-sacristia.com

PHOTOGRAPHS COURTESY OF MESÓN SACRISTÍA DE CAPUCHINAS.

Mesón Sacristia de la Compañia

With the opening of Mesón Sacristía de la Compañia, the Espinosa family has created a new niche of Mexican hotels—the antique gallery hotel—one of a few in the world, and definitely the best kind to stay in if you wish to experience all the historical grandeur of Puebla city. Famous for its colonial architecture, antiques and fine handicrafts, Puebla has undoubtedly become the antique mecca of Mexico. Historical treasures are spotted at every corner, frescoes depicting four centuries of history adorn the city, and the generous use of Talavera, hand-painted Spanish tiles, can be admired from many of the magnificently restored colonial buildings.

However, it is at Mesón Sacristía de la Compañia that you'll be seeing the best selection of antique furnishings the city has to offer. Live among them and at the end of your stay, choose to buy and ship them home if you so desire.

As you would rightly guess, the Espinosas were antique dealers before venturing into hospitality. With four generations in the trade, the family has managed to amass an admirable trove of fine furniture, tapestries, sculptures and religious art. These are artfully scattered around the hotel's 19th-century colonial

building that houses eight rooms, an award-winning restaurant and an antique gallery.

The décor is best described as eclectic with a homely, rustic touch. The traditional Talavera ceramics, spotted in many parts of Puebla, are used with gold leaves to provide exquisite detailing and pomp to the main areas. The hotel may be filled with antiques, but it dispels the cold museum feel through lacquered brick floors, colourful walls and brick-lined arches, all giving a vibrant lived-in atmosphere to the intimate boutique hotel.

Besides its fine artefacts, the other main attraction of la Compañia is its restaurant. Here, Pueblan specialities are served in a relaxed atmosphere, where a band strums Mexican folk tunes nightly. Select the most humble food of the region, the simple chanclas (bread rolls filled with sausages) or the delicate carne arriera (grilled beef with tequila), and you'll be rewarded with one of the best gastronomic experiences in the area.

THIS PAGE (FROM ABOVE): The antique gallery has paintings, sculptures and other treasures for sale; a brick archway and pastel-coloured walls lend a homely feel to the room.

OPPOSITE: Guests are instantly transported to 19th-century Mexico through the use of antiques and rustic furnishing.

FACTS

ROOMS	6 rooms • 2 suites
FOOD	Restaurant-bar Compañía: Pueblan
DRINK	El Confesionario: tequilas and Mexican cocktails
FEATURES	19th-century colonial building furnished with antiques • antique gallery
NEARBY	Puebla city • Los Sapos antiques market • El Parián crafts market
CONTACT	6 Sur 304, Callejón de los Sapos, Centro Histórico, Puebla 72000 • telephone: +1.800.712 4028 or +52.222 232 3554 • facsimile: +52.222 232 4513 • email: sacristia@mesones-sacristia.com • website: www.mesones-sacristia.com

CASA TAMAYO CUERNAVACA

THIS PAGE: *Rooms are designed with lots of white and cream paired with the clean lines of modern, wrought-iron furniture.*

OPPOSITE (CLOCKWISE FROM TOP LEFT): *Floor-to-ceiling glass windows and doors invite the mild sun into your living quarters; formerly the home of Mexican painter Rufino Tamayo, the hotel and its gardens still retain the air of a stately residence; Restaurant Tamayo specialises in the melding of Mexican and Italian flavours.*

It's hard to believe that Cuernavaca is only 45 minutes away from bustling Mexico City. Drive into this old town and everything changes: the architecture, the pace, the landscape, and even the weather. Resting at a much lower altitude than the capital, Cuernavaca enjoys a lush, semi-tropical environment with balmy, spring-like temperatures all year round. But besides its perfect climate, Cuernavaca is also famous for being deeply connected to its history.

It's impossible to walk for any length in this beautiful town without coming across one of Cuernavaca's palaces, walled villas, museums and classic haciendas. This capital state of Morelos was a retreat for royalty, from Aztec rulers to colonial emperors, and is now considered a cultural treasure for its role in the country's history.

Though the town may be undoubtedly pretty, it is the great outdoors that awes. Lush, wild and untouched, the landscape represents all that is unbridled about nature. East and southeast of Cuernavaca are two volcanoes—Ixaccihuatl and Popocatépetl—potent symbols of the earth's energy, and a constant reminder to visitors of the immense power of the land.

Visitors seeking the restorative energy of Cuernavaca's wild and rural outdoors do, however, have a choice of more-than-civilised housing options that are considered to be among Mexico's finest. Cuernavaca having been a holiday retreat for Mexicans and foreigners for centuries, now boasts the most elaborate and luxurious guesthouses. However, if you're seeking solitude amidst a more discreet setting just outside the busy zone of the town, there's CASA TAMAYO CUERNAVACA, found at the edge of tropical wilderness.

It is the perfect place to seek rest and revitalisation from the area's famous spring-like climate.

In an old pueblo where Emperor Maximilian, Malcolm Lowry and Erich Fromm lived, CASA TAMAYO CUERNAVACA nestles amid sun-dappled shadows and flowering trees filled with singing birds.

In this former house of painter Rufino Tamayo, artists and intellectual friends including writer Garcia Márquez, painter and cartoonist Abel Quezada, Queen Maria José di Savoia, actress Maria Felix, Mexican presidents and

many other personalities relaxed and recharged their creative energies. With its 12 exquisite rooms, an acclaimed restaurant and serene ambience, CASA TAMAYO CUERNAVACA remains an oasis of tranquillity for free spirits. It is the perfect place to seek rest and revitalisation from the area's famous spring-like climate. After all, if spring is when the earth experiences its rebirth, what better setting then for a personal renaissance?

PHOTOGRAPHS COURTESY OF CASA TAMAYO CUERNAVACA.

FACTS		
	ROOMS	12 rooms
	FOOD	Restaurant Tamayo: Mexican-Italian fusion
	DRINK	Bar La Cosa Nostra
	FEATURES	historical residence • 2 pools • gallery • fitness centre
	BUSINESS	meeting facilities for small groups
	NEARBY	Jardín Borda gardens • Teopanzolco Pyramid • Xochicalco ruins • Ixaccihuatl and Popocatépetl volcanoes • 2 golf courses • sports club with 8 tennis courts
	CONTACT	Rufino Tamayo 26, Colonia Acapatzingo, Cuernavaca, Morelos 62440 • telephone: +52.777 318 9477 • facsimile: +52.777 312 8186 • email: lasmusas@casatamayo.com.mx • website: www.casatamayo.com.mx

Quinta las Acacias

To the indigenous tribes, Guanajuato was Quanax-juato (Place of Frogs), because its mountainous terrain was so formidable, they believed it was only inhabitable to frogs. A few centuries later, the Spanish found rich veins of silver in Guanajuato, which they extracted to produce great fortunes and built a magnificent town on the site.

Today, the mountains are considered to be an important characteristic of the area—a dramatic backdrop against the quaint town of Guanajuato, with its elaborate network of cobblestone alleys, streets, tunnels, and sophisticated European architecture. It was among the richest cities in Mexico during the colonial era, and many of its grandest cathedrals, mansions, theatres and monuments were built between the 16th and 18th centuries. It is perhaps the most European and picturesque city in the country, and has recently been recognised as a World Heritage Site.

At boutique hotel Quinta las Acacias, guests can fully immerse themselves in the elegant colonial ambience of the city. They can take part in the many festivities around the plazas and be awed by the dramatic landscape that surrounds them.

Built in the 19th century, the French-style residence of Quinta las Acacias is located in one of the city's finest neighbourhoods, steps away from the vibrant town square. More interestingly, the hotel itself is built against the base of a mountain, ensuring magnificent views at a surprisingly close range. Its architecture makes the best use of the surroundings with some of the nine suites leading to terraces directly facing the mountain. There is even an outdoor jacuzzi for optimum indulgence.

This former home of a wealthy family is thoroughly European in design, featuring French windows, Spanish arches, wooden and marble floors, and 14 wrought-iron

THIS PAGE (CLOCKWISE FROM TOP):
Classic French architecture is given a modern twist; savour fine Mexican cuisine at the quaint dining room; balconies open out to views of the nearby park.
OPPOSITE: *An outdoor jacuzzi on the terrace provides relaxation in the sun.*

...guests can fully immerse themselves in the elegant colonial ambience of the city.

balconies that overlook the Florencio Antillon Park. The rooms are luxuriously decorated with European furnishings and given cheerful Mexican touches. This award-winning hotel is today a member of Mexico Boutique Hotels.

Within walking distance are the treasures of the city—theatres, cathedrals, the Diego Rivera Museum, and the famous Callejón del Beso (Alley of the Kiss)—a network of alleyways so narrow that lovers each standing on a balcony on either side can reach across the alley to exchange a kiss. After navigating the town by foot, guests can return to the hotel for superb Mexican fare—traditional dishes such as enjococadas (corn bread filled with beans) and poblana (zucchini and mushroom) soup given a dose of French flair.

With its elegant European architecture, warm service and fine food, Quinta las Acacias is certainly the most enjoyable way to relive the splendour of Guanajuato.

PHOTOGRAPHS COURTESY OF QUINTA LAS ACACIAS.

FACTS

ROOMS	5 European suites • 3 Mexican suites with jacuzzis • 1 master suite
FOOD	Quinta las Acacias Restaurant: Mexican
DRINK	Quinta las Acacias Bar
FEATURES	outdoor jacuzzi • gardens • library
BUSINESS	Internet access
NEARBY	Florencio Antillon Park • Diego Rivera Museum • Callejón del Beso (Alley of the Kiss)
CONTACT	Paseo de la Presa 168, Guanajuato 36000 • telephone: +52.473 731 1517 • fascimile: +52.473 731 1862 • email: acacias@int.com.mx • website: www.quintalasacacias.com.mx or www.mexicoboutiquehotels.com/lasacacias

pacificcoast

Nuevo León

Durango

Zacatecas

Tamaulipas

San Luis Potosi

Gulf of Mexico

Aguascalientes

Nayarit

> Four Seasons Resort
Punta Mita
Punta de Mita •
Bahía de Banderas
Yelapa • Puerto Vallarta
> Verana

Guanajuato

Querétaro

Hidalgo

Jalisco

> Hotelito Desconocido • Cruz de Loreto

Mexico State

Tlaxcala
Mexico City

Barra de Navidad • • Cihuatlán
> El Careyes Beach Resort
> El Tamarindo Golf Resort
Colima

Michoacán

Morelos

Puebla

Veracruz

• Ixtapa
> Villa del Sol — • Zihuatanejo

Guerrero

Pacific Ocean

Oaxaca

• Pie de la Cuesta
> Las Brisas Acapulco — • Acapulco

the other riviera

Mexico's extensive Pacific coastline, stretching from the south of Mazatlán to Chiapas, is home to the many first-class resorts and beaches that have given this country its reputation as a holiday-maker's paradise. Stunning coastal scenery, wooded mountains and enchanting seaside villages provide the backdrop to hideaways large and small, in the legendary resort towns of Puerto Vallarta, Acapulco and Zihuatanejo.

Geographically described as the Central Pacific Coast, these 850 miles (1,368 km) of tropical paradise start where the Sea of Cortez ends—just 8 miles (13 km) south of the Tropic of Cancer. Collectively it is known as the Gold Coast or Mexican Riviera—not to be confused with the Riviera Maya on the east of the Caribbean. This endless coastline, with its rugged beauty and powerful surf, runs south from the seaside city and fishing port of Mazatlán in the southern state of Sinaloa, down to Acapulco in Guerrero.

It seems little is known of pre-Hispanic Pacific coast cultures in comparison with those of the Aztecs, the Purépecha or the Mayan civilisations. Visitors to the hotels along the coast, however, have not been the first to seek refuge here.

Although no major monuments were left behind, archaeological finds show that when the Spaniards invaded Bahía de Acapulco (Bay of Acapulco) in 1512, an Indian tribe, the predecessors to the Aztecs, had been living around the area and the nearby Bahía de Puerto Marqués (Bay of Puerto Marqués) for about 2,000 years. They were enslaved and displaced from their homeland by 1550 when Spanish settlements were established and colonisation began.

Manzanillo was Spanish conquistador Hernán Cortés' first choice for the continent's gateway to the Orient, although Acapulco, with its large natural harbour, finally became the region's major port. In 1523, Cortés and merchants joined forces to finance a trade route between Mexico City and Acapulco, known as the Camino de Asia.

As the only port in the New World authorised to receive Spanish trading ships from the Philippines and China, Acapulco's trade with Asia flourished on a large scale. As a result of the economic boom, its population increased, as did its wealth, and this newly founded city soon became an important trading centre between Asia and Spain.

PAGE 128: Romantic sunsets and a warm climate continue to draw thousands to the Pacific coast.

THIS PAGE (FROM TOP): A local fisherman bringing in his catch; lobsters freshly hauled from the sea.

OPPOSITE: Los Arcos in Puerto Vallarta, sculpted by the powerful waves of the Pacific.

Superb coastal scenery, wooded mountains and enchanting seaside villages provide the backdrop to the hideaways...

Lured by the prospect of wealth, Dutch and English pirate ships swarmed the Pacific coast in the 17th century. To ward off pirates in Acapulco, a pentagonal fort, the Fuerte de San Diego, was built atop a hill overlooking the Bahía de Acapulco in 1616. Today, panoramic views of Acapulco can still be enjoyed from this beautifully restored fort. It now houses the history museum, Museo Histórico de Acapulco, which showcases exhibits detailing the city's history.

In Zihuatanejo (Place of Women), ancient stone carvings, figurines and ceramics suggest that its bay area was home to civilisations dating as far back as the Olmecs. Lying opposite Zihuatanejo is Playa Las Gatas, which was once the playground of ancient royalty. Legend has it that Calzontzín, one of the last Tarascan kings from Michoacán, built a stone reef in the waters to keep the waves down. Till this day, the reef still protects the beach. Coral has since grown onto the rocks, now known as King's Reef, a habitat for tropical fish and a safe place for children to snorkel and swim in.

Other beaches around Zihuatanejo Bay also have their names rooted in the past. Like Acapulco and other fishing villages along the Pacific coastline, Zihuatanejo was a popular stopover for long voyages and a haven for Spanish fleets, pirates and explorers. The beautiful Playa La Ropa (Beach of Clothes), for instance, got its name from the silk washed ashore from a wrecked Spanish ship.

new world resort

Puerto Vallarta, in the state of Jalisco, was formerly a fishing village that was transformed into a sophisticated resort city in the 1960s. It shot to fame when Richard Burton and Elizabeth Taylor landed here for the filming of 'The Night of the Iguana'.

This prime stretch of coast from the Bahía de Banderas (Bay of Flags) to the town of Barra de Navidad, was christened Costa Alegre (Happy Coast) in the 1980s, and spans 200 miles (322 km). Set against the amazing Sierra Madre mountains and dense rainforests, Puerto Vallarta bustles with internationally acclaimed art galleries, trendy boutiques, cosmopolitan bars and restaurants.

THIS PAGE (FROM TOP): *The peaceful waters of Nueva Vallarta's marina belie what the town has to offer.*

OPPOSITE: *Sea and sunset views from a private pool at Villa del Sol in Guerrero.*

But despite its posh hotels, sizzling nightlife and commercial centres, Puerto Vallarta still maintains an Old World mystique with its maze of cobblestone streets, red tiled roofs and white adobe buildings. Sleepy fishing towns of Mismaloya, Mascota and Talpa punctuate the coastline, offering visitors a glimpse into the real Puerto Vallarta—the way it was and the way it has remained until today.

Travellers with a thirst for adventure and exploration will find plenty of specialised tours and activities. There are visits to ruins, mountain expeditions, hiking, scuba diving, horseback riding, bungee jumping, hot air balloon rides, whale-watching tours, and championship golf. There are also over 40 beaches snaking from Punta Mita and Los Veneros in the north, to the more isolated beaches of Quimixto and Yelapa in the south.

One of the most attractive features of Puerto Vallarta is that it is a melting pot of social activities and cultures, as well as a few exclusive hotels which you can retreat to, away from the city's bustle. Both picturesque in setting and diverse in appeal, the romantic, colonial city of Puerto Vallarta has long served as a tranquil refuge for those seeking more than just a quiet beach vacation.

playground of the glitterati

Named after Vicente Guerrero, the second president of Mexico, the mountainous and arid state of Guerrero is one of Mexico's poorest. The word 'Guerrero' also means 'warrior', an appropriate name because of the state's long-standing tradition of blood feuds amongst some of its isolated communities.

The towns of Acapulco and Zihuatanejo are well worth a day trip. For those who are curious enough to venture into the soul of Mexico's coastal resorts, Acapulco is the place to go. Awash with the nostalgia of its glory days in the 1950s, the city is a refreshing contrast to the sterility of modern-day beach resorts.

Acapulco began its transformation to that of a premier resort destination in the 1920s, when the Prince of Wales visited the bay on a fishing expedition. The construction of the airport followed in 1928 and this fuelled the beginning of Acapulco's glamorous jet-set whirl to fame. Soon wealthy Mexicans, American writers, Hollywood stars and

THIS PAGE: *Puerto Vallarta's architectural style fuses rural settings with modern buildings.*

OPPOSITE (FROM TOP): *The majestic gold interior of the Santa Prisca Cathedral in Taxco, Guerrero; the best way to see the town is to hop on a city tram.*

the European glitterati flocked to Acapulco. It was here that Elizabeth Taylor married Mike Todd, and celebrities like Frank Sinatra and Judy Garland became regular visitors.

The weather is a major draw—warm waters and year-round sunshine provide a romping ground for those who love the outdoors. One attraction not to be missed is the legendary clavadista or cliff diver who performs daredevil antics at La Quebrada. You can catch at least three divers performing at each show, swan diving from jaw-dropping heights of up to 148 ft (45 m) into the tumultuous ocean swells below.

When the sun goes down, the nights come alive with 24-hour fun. Most of the nightclubs, bars, major hotels and restaurants are centred around the pulsating La Costera—Acapulco's most celebrated enclave of revelry. These truly lavish clubs can be as exclusive and elaborate as those in New York or Los Angeles.

Acapulco can be an unforgettable experience for travellers seeking glitzy nightlife, but if you prefer somewhere more secluded, the city has another secret that Mexicans are still wary of sharing. Ten miles (16 km) northwest, a 25-minute drive along a winding road where the ocean sparkles with a pristine glow, lies Pie de la Cuesta.

Here, a long, narrow strip of land separates the thundering Pacific Ocean from the freshwater, mangrove-fringed Laguna de Coyuca. The lagoon is three times the size of Acapulco Bay and fantastic for swimming. Water-skiing and horseback riding on the beach are also popular.

bay watch

Much further up the coast from Acapulco, about 400 miles (644 km) south of the port town of Manzanillo in Colima, lies one of the most pristine hideaways in the country. Zihuatanejo (pronounced as 'zee-wah-ta-neh-ho') has a sheltered bay of astounding beauty and size. Its mellow coastal atmosphere, fresh seafood and desolate beaches have long made it a favourite for those in the know.

Most activities in this unspoiled seaside village are water-oriented. Waves are gentle on all of its beaches, including Playa Madera, Playa Municipal and Playa Majahua. Horse riders and sunset watchers enjoy the broad, sandy beach lined with restaurants and rustic hotels, making it a soothing departure from the city's bright lights.

Not too far from the beaches, the downtown shopping district and artisan markets are bordered by Playa Principal, where you will find Mexican handicrafts, ceramics, Taxco silver, wood carvings, leather and masks in abundance from all over Guerrero. Bargaining is all part of the fun here. The Mercado Turístoco la Marina on Cinco de Mayo has the most stalls for souvenirs, while more shopping can be found in Cuauhtémoc, and the Mercado Municipal de las Artesanías on González, near Juárez.

Sea turtles too, are a common sight in Zihuatanejo and you may even spot whales during mating season. In between snorkelling and surfing, stop for lunch at some of the finer beaches further west beyond Punta Ixtapa. This is a sure way to get sunburnt, so sun block, long sleeves and hats are absolutely essential.

THIS PAGE (FROM TOP): Speedboats pound the coast of Acapulco Bay; a cliff diver leaps boldly into the waves between the narrow rocks of La Quebrada.

OPPOSITE (FROM TOP): Acapulco's 'Costera' is famous for its strip of hotels, restaurants and bars that runs parallel to the coast; seashells embedded in the yellow grainy sand of Acapulco's beaches.

sun, surf + snow

From February to April, Californian grey whales bear their young in Bahía de Banderas (Bay of Banderas), the seventh largest bay in the world. With a 110-mile (177-km) shoreline and a depth of a mile (2 km), the bay was supposedly formed by the sunken crater of a gigantic, extinct volcano.

Despite the abundance of prey, the bay is practically shark-free because of the large dolphin colony breeding here. Adult dolphins patrol the bay's entrance to protect their young. Giant manta rays also inhabit the bay and can be seen leaping over the waters during mating season in April. If you are out on a boat, you may even spot humpback whales as they gather to mate or bear calves from November to March.

Four different species of sea turtles lay their eggs on the 17 golden beaches of Costa Careyes, located between Puerto Vallarta and Manzanillo. Visitors to the area can participate in turtle-protection programmes from June to October. In a typical visit, guests trek to Teopa Beach to search for hatchlings that they can release into the sea. They also learn how to incubate nesting turtles to a protected area to lay their eggs.

Offshore, black and green iguanas can be spotted combing the grounds, and pelicans can be sighted hunting for fish close to the shore. As the Pacific coast is known for its multitude of bird species, bird-watching tours to local sanctuaries and forests are major highlights. Joining a deep-sea fishing expedition is another exhilarating option, particularly in places like Manzanillo and Zihuatanejo, where you have a good chance of returning with marlin, swordfish or sailfish for your next meal.

Those who expect the Pacific coast to be all sun and surf are surprised by the states of Sinaloa, Nayarit, Jalisco, Colima and Guerrero, where mountains, volcanoes, forests, lagoons and farmland preside. For adventurers who can tear themselves away from the ocean, the towering Sierra Madre Occidental and Sierra Madre Sur mountain ranges are great for hiking and climbing.

Just north of Colima city, the national park of Nevado de Colima is where the Volcán de Fuego (Fire Volcano) rests, while five-and-a-half miles away, the extinct Volcán Nevado de Colima is a hiker's paradise with its snowy 12,790-ft (3,898-m) summit.

THIS PAGE (FROM TOP): *A cascading waterfall hidden in a cave; to catch sight of a whale's tail is considered good luck in Pacific coast culture.*
OPPOSITE: *Pelicans can be found gracing both the east and west coastlines of the Pacific.*

...the bay was supposedly formed by the sunken crater of a gigantic, extinct volcano.

El Careyes Beach Resort

El Careyes Beach Resort is a modern and elegant interpretation of Mexico's resort-by-the-sea. Forty-eight rooms and three casitas are built in a crescent curve along the wide and pristine expanse of beach, each a spirited blend of Mexican and Mediterranean styles, with boldly coloured walls paired with Mexican tiles, modern furnishings and artworks.

Unlike the typical Mexican beach, however, serenity reigns with the Pueblan-style buildings coddled by dramatic cliffs—a seemingly formidable barrier to the distractions of the outside world. Here, delights are simple and rustic, with much enjoyment derived from the biological diversity of the area. Surrounded by tropical forest-covered hills, guests can engage in some serious birdwatching for some of the most exotic species in the world. Or simply enjoy a walk through the gardens for a colourful showcase of indigenous tropical flowers and palms.

At certain times of the year, guests can also witness the birth of turtles right on their beach—a miracle that takes place just steps from their rooms.

In line with the theme of simple pleasures, rooms are stylishly pared down. Earthy Mexican tiles decorate each room,

THIS PAGE (CLOCKWISE FROM TOP):
The poolside terrace for lounging any time of the day; the resort is structured like a horseshoe so that every suite has generous views of the pool; rooms are decked in soothing pastel hues contrasted with bright earthy flooring.
OPPOSITE: Luxuriate in the privacy of your own petal-filled pool while taking in the beauty of the sea.

and drama is added to the pastel-coloured abode by vividly hued pillows and bedspreads. There are also suites that offer guests moments of solitude with the full amenities of a residence with a dining room, kitchenette and jacuzzi. There are also aspects of pure indulgence such as the private pools in the suites and the spectacular view of the Pacific Ocean from every room.

Though many of the guests may choose El Careyes for isolation, they can also enjoy the services the resort offers. There's the spa with a full range of facials, body treatments and massages. For the more energetic, there's a host of water activities available at the hotel, including snorkelling, fishing or kayaking, that provide a complete immersion in the resort's glorious surroundings.

But ultimately, total relaxation rules, and there are many little niches around the resort that offer opportunities for undisturbed lounging and basking—on a deck chair with fine sand on your feet, at the poolside terrace, by its swim-up bar and déli, or on the terrace outside your room with unobstructed views of the green hills.

Idyllic days end with the sumptuous cooking of resident chef, Patricia Quintana, at Lantana Restaurant. Quintana, author of the cookbook, *The Cuisine of the Water Gods*, pays tribute to Mexico's rich supply and variety of seafood with dishes that are refreshingly simple. At the ocean-front tables, exquisite meals and impeccable service provide the perfect finale.

FACTS

ROOMS	29 rooms • 19 suites • 3 casitas
FOOD	Lantana Restaurant: coastal Mexican • swim-up déli at pool: snacks
DRINK	Lantana Bar • swim-up bar at pool
FEATURES	2 tennis courts • gym • spa • outdoor jacuzzi • pool • private pools in some suites
BUSINESS	meeting and events facilities
NEARBY	Tamarindo Golf Course • Cuitzmala • Melaque • Barra de Navidad • Manzanillo city • Puerto Vallarta
CONTACT	Carrertera km 53.5, Barra de Navidad, Costa Careyes, Jalisco 48983 • telephone: +52.315 351 0000 • facsimile: +52.315 351 0100 • email: careyes@grupoplan.com • website: www.starwood.com/careyes

El Tamarindo Golf Resort

El Tamarindo Golf Resort is so ideally situated between a glorious ocean and a dense forest that it's impossible to get a bad view at any angle. Guests do have a chance, however, to select what they would like to face when they wake up—a vista of blue ocean or an expanse of tropical green foliage. The 29 stand-alone villas that are dispersed on the 2,049-acre (829-hectare) ecological reserve along Mexico's Pacific Coast are divided into different categories that denote their location—Beachfront, Palm Tree, Garden and Forest.

THIS PAGE (CLOCKWISE FROM RIGHT):
Meditate or enjoy a massage under a rustic pavilion; thatched roofs and hammocks are contrasted with modern, luxurious furnishing.
OPPOSITE: The seamless, palm-fringed pool meets the expanse of the Pacific Ocean and brilliant blue sky.

All are spacious and luxurious with dark wood floors, palapa-thatched roofs and crisp white linen. What's more, the suites cleverly meld the indoors and out, with terraces that lead guests to personal plunge and splash pools. Guests can also head out to the garden hammocks on balmy afternoons and doze off to the sound of crashing waves or the stirring of jungle animals.

Of course, El Tamarindo's surroundings are naturally spectacular. Nestled in Tenacitita Bay, a serene cove which hugs the Pacific Coast and is bound by a strip of almost virgin jungle, the setting is perhaps the closest guests can get to Eden. But while these 'amenities' are bestowed by nature, there's plenty that's man-made and equally

...doze off to the sound of crashing waves or the stirring of jungle animals.

exquisite. The resort's gracious service, fine facilities and understated luxury ensure that it is the ultimate holiday indulgence.

There are many activities for pampered guests to enjoy at El Tamarindo. For one, there's the private 18-hole championship golf course designed by David Fleming and Robert Trent Jones Jr., which offers a challenging game as it carefully respects the natural contours and features of the land. Golfers are blissfully shaded by a forest of palms, and are able to enjoy, undisturbed by other players, the peaceful course that faces the ocean.

After a day on the greens, guests can ease away muscle fatigue and soothe tanned skin with a range of massages, body treatments and facials at El Tamarindo's fully-equipped spa. At this point, guests are usually inebriated with complete relaxation, but if there're any vestiges of stress left, a two-and-a-half hour Temazcal treatment—a

pre-Hispanic cleansing ritual that involves a mud wrap and a sea bath—should thoroughly appease them.

Tamarindo Restaurant overlooks the pool, beach and sea, and serves up a daily menu featuring the creations of author and chef, Patricia Quintana. Many of her specialities are in her book, *The Cuisine of the Water Gods.*

Once, not too long ago, El Tamarindo was a by-invitation-only destination for the owner's guests. Ever since it has been acquired by Starwood Hotels and Resorts as part of its Luxury Collection, it has hosted the most discerning travellers from around the world, and is finally receiving all the recognition it truly deserves.

FACTS		
ROOMS	29 villas	
FOOD	Tamarindo Restaurant: eclectic regional and coastal Mexican	
DRINK	Tamarindo Bar: cocktails and snacks	
FEATURES	ecological reserve • 18-hole championship golf course • 2 tennis courts • spa • pool • plunge and splash pools in all suites • personal butler • free non-motorised water sports	
BUSINESS	meeting and event facilities	
NEARBY	Manzanillo city • Puerto Vallarta • Cuitzmala • Melaque • Barra de Navidad	
CONTACT	Carretera Melaque y Puerto Vallarta km 7.5, Cihuatlán, Jalisco 48970 • telephone: +52.315 351 5032 • facsimile: +52.315 351 5070 • email: tamarindo@grupoplan.com • website: www.luxurycollection.com	

Four Seasons Resort Punta Mita

THIS PAGE: The sprawling infinity pool overlooks the Pacific coast.

OPPOSITE (FROM TOP): The resort offers 140 rooms and suites located in one-, two- and three-storey casitas; a Zen-like water feature provides passers-by with moments of calm and cool.

Expectations of the first Four Seasons Resort in Mexico are naturally high. And in the case of Punta Mita, they have certainly been met and exceeded. Then again, it's hard to go wrong with such a location— 1,500 acres (607 hectares) of lush greenery bordered on three sides by the ocean and neighbour to jungle-covered mountains. Natural settings just don't get more spectacular than this. Seclusion is almost a guarantee, the resort being 45 minutes away from the nearest town. And despite the allure of the calm, warm waters of Banderas Bay, beautiful beaches and balmy weather, it has remained remarkably 'undiscovered'. Not too long ago, the only inhabitants of the area were fishermen; electricity and telephone lines were a

relatively new introduction; and with the resort's eco-friendly development, the bay still remains host to turtles, manta rays and the rarely spotted humpback whale.

As a hideaway, Four Seasons Resort Punta Mita is unbeatable. With its selection of dining and relaxation options, there's no need for guests to venture out. They'll be so thoroughly pampered, it'll be hard to think of places beyond the resort. And it's not just the prerequisites of a Mexican beach holiday—ocean activities and memorable sunsets—that guests enjoy.

There's the stunning Jack Nicklaus golf course with a special over-the-water hole to provide unforgettable drives; the large infinity pool on the cliff side with views of the beach below; and the European spa that's heavenly to lose oneself in for a complete day. And of course, all the other additions that make a Four Seasons hotel what it is: grand lobbies, elegant rooms, luxurious details and gracious service.

Fans of the luxury hotel brand should not, however, expect a glamorous city edition on a beach. The entire resort is designed to give a deeper appreciation of where you are in Mexico rather than just surround you with Four Seasons luxury—although that is more than apparent. With

red tiled roofs, dark wood furniture, patios and terraces, the rooms evoke the ambience of a cosy, well-designed Mexican home. And because this is tequila country, the cultural centre offers tequila tastings and language lessons, as well as talks on local crafts and traditions.

The centrepiece of the resort, however, is the 19-hole (one hole is on a natural

island) world-class course. The layout is naturally dazzling, with portions of holes on the Pacific and others skirting Banderas Bay. Along the way, golfers are shaded with 1,800 palms which form part of the green landscape. These however, are in danger of being eclipsed by the last hole on the Tail of the Whale—an atoll of rock, named as such because of its unique shape—just under 200 yd (183 m) from shore. Braving the onshore breeze while attempting to reach the generous green that beckons from the sea is the ultimate challenge.

For the meek-hearted who would rather give the golfing challenge a miss, the fitness centre is large and professionally equipped, and there are four tennis courts on its grounds. Sybaritic guests should not miss out on Apauane Spa—a cool, white temple of spa pleasures with an endless list of massages, facials and treatments. The emphasis is very much on treatments based on the traditions and culture of the Huichol Indians. Try the tequila and sage oil massage, or the Temaztac wrap, a Mayan treatment that softens and smoothens skin. There are golf-spa packages to address sporting problems, and sun-seekers' treatments that prep the body before a day of basking.

Or else, there are always the infinitely comfortable rooms where guests can while away their time leisurely. In true Four Seasons style, beds are massive and plush, and baths deep and carved of marble. Most suites offer plunge pools, and separate sitting rooms, bars and powder rooms.

Despite the exclusivity of the place, family holidays are welcomed and encouraged. Two- and three-bedroom suites are available, and children are kept busy with the Kids-For-All-Seasons programme

which offers activities such as hiking, painting and ceramic classes.

That leaves relieved parents free to enjoy the vast dining options available at the hotel. The stylish Aramara restaurant features Chino-Latino cuisine, which fuses Mexican, Cuban, Columbian and Caribbean flavours. Nuna Bar, overlooking the ocean, specialises in ceviche, which is undoubtedly the best way to enjoy the fresh seafood of the area. Guests are even allowed to pick their catch from the fishermen who arrive at noon.

And the hotel's location simply enhances the whole Mexican experience. Blessed not only with the best beaches, the town is also a centre of history and art. The only caveat: guests probably won't leave Four Seasons Resort Punta Mita long enough to find out.

THIS PAGE: The world-renowned 19-hole golf course is designed by Jack Nicklaus.

OPPOSITE (FROM TOP): For romantic interludes, dinner can be served on a rocky outcrop above the ocean accompanied by a trio of musicians; Four Seasons-style luxury is apparent the moment you step into the grand lobby.

FACTS		
ROOMS	114 rooms • 26 suites	
FOOD	Aramara: Chino-Latino • Nuna Bar: seafood • Ketsi: regional Mexican and Californian • Tail of the Whale (at Golf Club House): international	
DRINK	Nuna Bar • Lobby Lounge	
FEATURES	golf course • heated pool • cultural centre • fitness centre • spa • 4 tennis courts	
BUSINESS	event and conference facilities	
NEARBY	Puerto Vallarta • beach	
CONTACT	Punta Mita, Bahía de Banderas, Nayarit 63734 • telephone: +52.329 191 6000 • facsimile: +52.329 291 6060 • email: res.puntamita@fourseasons.com • website: www.fourseasons.com	

PHOTOGRAPHS COURTESY OF FOUR SEASONS RESORT PUNTA MITA.

Hotelito Desconocido

THIS PAGE: Located within a tropical estuary, the resort brings guests closer to nature.

OPPOSITE (FROM LEFT): A palapa roof, wooden floors and antiques bring out the rustic details of each guestroom; Mexican favourites are served at El Cantarito.

Italian fashion designer Marcello Murzilli is a man who certainly doesn't do things in halves. When he sold his multi-million-dollar company, he spent the next two years searching for the most idyllic site for his next project, an eco-luxury resort. His travels took him to Mexico where he came across 40 miles (64 km) of pristinely preserved land nestled between the Sierra Madre Mountains and the Pacific Ocean.

This is where he began work on Hotelito Desconocido, or 'little unknown hotel', located within the El Ermitaño estuary. It has since become everything Murzilli had imagined it to be—a resort that is truly friendly to the environment without compromising on the standards of five-star luxury.

The very concept of a luxury hotel with all its modern trappings—electricity, telephones, flashy restaurants and buzzing nightlife—are glaringly absent from Hotelito Desconocido. Instead, these are replaced with solar-powered ceiling fans, solar-heated water, recycled products, hand-made toiletries and a restaurant that serves organic food.

When it comes to romancing its guests, Hotelito Desconocido scores in ingenuity. Come evening, the resort, rooms and pathways are lit by the soft glow of candles and torches, while outdoor bamboo baths allow you to relax amidst a tropical garden.

With a generous dose of creativity, Hotelito Desconocido has an inventive system for room service that makes up for its lack of telephones. From the comfort of your bed, you may summon for coffee by simply pulling a rope. This hoists a flag, signalling that you are ready to be served.

The hotel is able to provide such intimate hospitality because of its small size.

There are no telephones to silence, no televisions to switch off...

It has just 29 rooms or palafitos—indigenous bungalows perched on stilts over a lagoon. Each palafito revels in its own distinctive décor and style, modelled after the Mexican lottery, a type of bingo game that uses images rather than numbers.

Look out of your private terrace and you'll be treated to either views of the ocean, or the breathtaking 99-acre (40-hectare) nature reserve. Built in harmony with its natural environment, the resort blends seamlessly into the landscape with its palapa roofs and wooden floors.

More than 150 species of birds live on the land surrounding Hotelito Desconocido. Rowboat tours take you deeper into the estuary's wildlife, or you may choose to watch sea turtles lay their eggs on the beach. End the day by riding a horse down this long stretch of sand. Those in search of more sensual sedation can opt for an organic massage from the 'primitive' luxury spa which uses indigenous ingredients in its treatments.

It is this sheer luxury within the wilderness where one can truly disconnect from reality. There are no telephones to silence, no televisions to switch off, no pollution or noise from the traffic to ignore—only tranquillity for those in search of seclusion. Here, relaxing is mandatory.

FACTS

ROOMS	12 beachfront palafitos • 8 suites • 5 rooms • 3 master suites • 1 presidential suite
FOOD	El Cantarito: Mexican (breakfast and dinner) • El Nopalito (lunch)
DRINK	El Nopalito: beach bar
FEATURES	El Ermitaño estuary • tropical gardens • spa • saltwater pool • bird-watching tours • turtle nests • kayaking • windsurfing • mountain biking
BUSINESS	La Islita and Nopalito for open-air events • translator • meeting facilities
NEARBY	beaches • nature reserve
CONTACT	Playon de Mismaloya, Natural Reserve, 60 miles (96 km) south of Puerto Vallarta • telephone: +52.322 222 2526 • facsimile: +52.322 223 0293 • email: hotelito@hotelito.com • website: www.hotelito.com

PHOTOGRAPHS COURTESY OF HOTELITO DESCONOCIDO.

Verana

Don't expect to be mollycoddled for one minute when you're at Verana. Just to get to it is a bit of a trek—a 30-minute boat ride from Boca de Tomatlan beach and then a 10-minute hike by foot or on a mule, up the mountains. But all this hard work does increase your appreciation of the destination. Verana, a secret hideaway in the mountains of Valle de Sierra, is an inspiring piece of property; so seamlessly entrenched in the jungle that when you do finally arrive, your little hike just seems to add to the whole experience.

The hotel is undoubtedly as rustic as it gets when it comes to living in the jungle. Palapa, one of the most popular of its six houses, doesn't have windows and the rough stone walls are just waist-high. Guests can't be shy here and must get attuned to living with the occasional frog or butterfly seeking creature comforts in their quarters. Imagine a luxury camp, with the great outdoors around and overhead. Showers and baths are taken outdoors. And electricity is limited, so the hotel grounds are lit by torches and guests carry oil lamps to dinner (solar power keeps the kitchen going).

Despite its deliberately rough edges, Verana is intensely sophisticated. Rooms are as stylish as a modern art gallery. The magnificent infinity pool seems to float above the jungle. And the cuisine is so

refined, it could be served in the most elegant restaurants in New York. And yet, curiously, these trappings of comfort and luxury do seem to fit naturally into Verana's jungle environment. Look closely and you'll realise that the minimalist furniture, so modern and chic with its clean lines, is actually crafted out of indigenous wood from the jungle. Even what guests dine on is partially derived from its surroundings with the hotel's organic fruit plantation.

The creation of a husband-and-wife team, Heinz Legler, a famous Hollywood set designer, and Veronique Lievre, a prop stylist, Verana is perhaps their most dramatic piece of work yet. Set amid the cinematic scenery of the Pacific Ocean and Valle de Sierra mountains, their aim was to carve a home into the tropical jungle with all the ecological concerns in mind.

Residents of Verana have a choice to do as little or as much as they wish. A spa, built

into the rocky slopes of a mountain, offers treatments using native fresh fruit and plants. Or, discover the athlete within with jungle-trekking, mountain-biking and ocean-kayaking activities organised by the hotel.

At Verana, guests can achieve total relaxation and are enticed to experience the full splendour of their beautiful surroundings, yet be assured of a thoroughly sophisticated stay.

FACTS	
ROOMS	6 houses
FOOD	Verana restaurant: authentic Mexican • outdoor terrace: breakfast and dinner
DRINK	restaurant-bar
FEATURES	spring water pool • outdoor terrace for all rooms • spa • library
BUSINESS	telephone, facsimile and Internet services in Yelapa
NEARBY	Yelapa fishing village • Boca de Tomatlan beach • Bahía de Banderas • Marietta Islands for bird watching
CONTACT	Yelapa, Puerto Vallarta, Jalisco 48319 • telephone: +1.800.677 5156 (US) or +52.322 209 5107 • email: ana@verana.com website: www.verana.com

Las Brisas Acapulco

THIS PAGE: *Most casitas open out to beautiful outdoor terraces with private plunge pools.*

OPPOSITE (FROM TOP): *Seamless views of the hillside and Acapulco Bay from the terrace; the resort has an incredible selection of 210 pools.*

It's no wonder that the glamour and sophistication of Acapulco have been well immortalised in many Hollywood classics. Since the discovery of its golden beaches, Sierra Madre mountains, lagoons and tropical jungles in the 1920s, Acapulco has become a hotbed for movie stars and jet-setters. In fact, it is believed that Acapulco is the birthplace of Mexican tourism—from parasailing to swim-up bars, flashy hotels and all-night discos—it all began here.

The options of activities are limitless. Should one join the beautiful people on the beach, go on a safari, or relax by the beach bars along the coast? The best place to contemplate your choices is at Las Brisas Acapulco—a serene hotel perched on a hillside overlooking the bright lights of Acapulco Bay.

Only five minutes from the tourist zone of the city, and 15 minutes from the international airport, Las Brisas is just far enough to keep the bustle of Acapulco at arm's length, and yet close enough for you to explore should you wish to join the revelry.

Las Brisas is completely dedicated to privacy, making it an ideal place to rediscover the romance of Acapulco. Guests reside in individual casitas, spread over 110 acres (45 hectares) of lush vegetation. Most suites include a private pool and terrace; there are altogether 210 private pools at the guests' disposal.

Las Brisas has marble floors and mahogany woodwork that are in keeping with the classic feel of Acapulco. It also has an extensive setup of modern facilities: a gym, five tennis courts, a beauty salon and a spa which specialises in beauty therapy. A fleet of pink-and-white jeeps is available for ferrying guests around the resort.

Las Brisas is...an ideal place to rediscover the romance of Acapulco.

And of course, there's the gourmet food that sets the hotel apart as a five-star establishment. El Bella Vista, which soars over the bay, offers international favourites while diners enjoy an unending vista of the mountains, the Pacific Ocean, and sparkling city lights below. The private La Concha Beach Club with three large pools—one with a swim-up bar for midday flirtations—however, is where the heart of the hotel is, drawing guests to its fresh seafood restaurant. There is also the Déli-Shop for a quick bite should you wish to spend the afternoon exploring the area's natural landscape.

With the best of both worlds—stunning natural scenery and world-class nightlife—Acapulco has drawn the wealthiest and most famous travellers from around the world to its shores. And now, there's one more reason to head for Acapulco: the privacy and romance of Las Brisas.

FACTS		
	ROOMS	185 casitas with pools • 48 Brisas Beach Club casitas • 32 suites
	FOOD	El Bella Vista: international • La Concha Beach Club: seafood and grill • Déli-Shop
	DRINK	Bella Vista • Sunset Bar • Pool Bar
	FEATURES	210 pools • 5 tennis courts • gym • spa • shops • 24-hour medical services
	BUSINESS	meeting rooms for 10 to 280 people • audio-visual equipment • Internet access
	NEARBY	restaurants • golf course • shopping malls • Chapel of Peace • Puerto Marqués • international airport
	CONTACT	Carretera Escénica 5255, Fraccionamiento Las Brisas, Acapulco, Guerrero 39867 • telephone: +52.744 469 6900 • facsimile: +52.744 446 5328 • email: brisa@brisas.com.mx • website: www.brisas.com.mx

PHOTOGRAPHS COURTESY OF LAS BRISAS ACAPULCO.

Villa del Sol

Despite all the beautiful beaches that line the coast of Mexico, the sight of a fisherman with his morning's catch remains a fantasy. To discover the country the way it used to be—rustic, laid back and serene—come to Zihuatanejo and stay at Villa del Sol, a tribute to relaxation, Mexican style.

The property lies along Playa la Ropa, one of the prettiest and longest private beaches on Mexico's Pacific Riviera. With great foresight, owner Helmut Leins predicted that Playa la Ropa would make an enticing site for an intimate and exclusive beach resort. And that was before any hotelier had set sights upon it. Being the first meant that Villa del Sol had the pick of the coast—a mile- (2-km-) long stretch of crescent-shaped beach lined with palm trees and framed by crystal blue waters.

Since 1978, Villa del Sol has grown from just a handful of casitas into a 70-room-and-suite resort which has lost none of its incredible charm and cheerfulness. A miniature, blue-tiled river meanders through the premise, burbling happily in waterfalls and fountains before ending its route in a mirror-still lagoon. The grounds consist of abundant greenery, stand-alone two-storey casitas and four large swimming pools. An authentic Mexican abode buried in a luxuriant tropical forest.

The rooms are posh and pampering without being pretentious. Sponge-painted in the colours of tropical cocktails, the

An authentic Mexican abode buried in a luxuriant tropical forest.

individually decorated units combine local crafts with African and Asian touches. Indigenous materials are used as well to present Mexico living at its best.

Despite its casual approach, the requisite luxury touches are still there: Frette bed linen, native marble and private infinity pools for all suites. What's most striking is the immense charm of the rooms which meld Mayan and Mediterranean features—ideal for a laid-back seaside location—and yet achieves the ultimate standards of five-star indulgence.

Dining concepts are in line with the hotel's lifestyle. Restaurant at Villa del Sol serves Pacific-Mexican cuisine, while the alfresco La Cantina Bar and Grill offers Mediterranean favourites from an open kitchen. Both offer unbeatable views of the ocean. You can even choose to dine on the beach, where tables complete with silver and linen are laid out. And if you're early enough, you could possibly catch the elusive fisherman at work, with his neatly bundled morning catch which might just end up on your plate that evening.

FACTS		
	ROOMS	35 rooms • 35 suites
	FOOD	Restaurant at Villa del Sol: Pacific-Mexican • La Cantina Bar and Grill: Mexican and Mediterranean
	DRINK	La Cantina Bar and Grill
	FEATURES	4 pools • 2 tennis courts • private pools for all suites • spa • fitness centre
	BUSINESS	meeting facilities for small groups
	NEARBY	2 golf courses • Zihuatanejo fishing village
	CONTACT	Playa la Ropa s/n, Zihuatanejo, Guerrero 40880 • telephone: +52.755 555 5500 • facsimile: +52.755 554 2758 • email: reservation@hotelvilladelsol.net • website: www.hotelvilladelsol.net

PHOTOGRAPHS COURTESY OF VILLA DEL SOL.

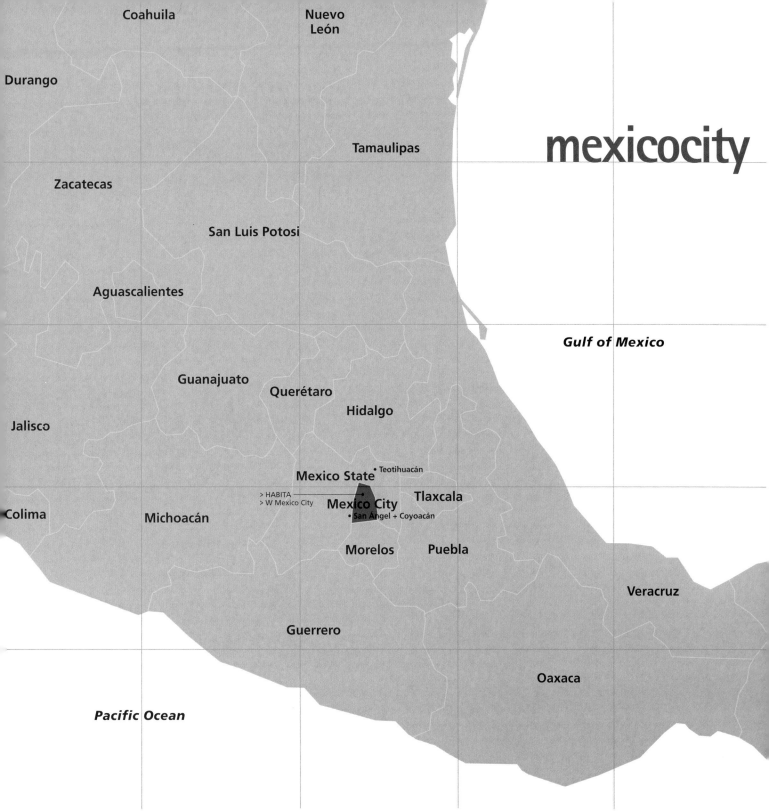

mexicocity

Coahuila

Nuevo León

Durango

Tamaulipas

Zacatecas

San Luis Potosi

Aguascalientes

Gulf of Mexico

Guanajuato

Querétaro

Hidalgo

Jalisco

• Teotihuacán

Mexico State

> HABITA
> W Mexico City

Mexico City

Tlaxcala

Colima

Michoacán

• San Ángel + Coyoacán

Morelos

Puebla

Veracruz

Guerrero

Oaxaca

Pacific Ocean

city chic

When you land in Mexico City at night, make sure you have a window seat. You will spy a sea of lights—streets and buildings glittering like a thousand diamond tiaras below—masked by occasional stretches of darkness, when the plane flies over a mountain or wasteland. The downward glide goes on for what feels like forever, then there is a dark shadow, another hill, and the shiny welcome parade continues.

It is an exciting descent into a highly energised city whose greater area, including the Valle de México (Valley of Mexico), teems with 22 million souls, a quarter of Mexico's population. Nearly everyone leaves the city with a very different opinion of Latin America's largest capital from that which they harboured on arrival.

The reason why expectations fall short of the offerings is that in many parts of the world, Mexico City is better known for its smog and overpopulation than for its world-class museums, nearby pyramids, complex cuisine and brisk nightlife. But its notoriety is fading in the light of what more and more people are discovering for themselves in the city. The world's eyes are on Mexico as a traveller's paradise.

Referred to locally as D.F. or Distrito Federal (Federal District), the city is a true microcosm of the country, presenting different faces and styles of Mexico. Reminders of past civilisations pervade the city alongside a multitude of contradictions: sleepy houses and modern hotels, slums and skyscrapers, music and noise.

As a hip travel destination, Mexico City has always been an exuberant mêlée of top restaurants, non-stop nightlife, fine art, parades and fiestas, set against the backdrop of colonial churches, ruined Aztec temples and sleek buildings. But now, its more frenzied attractions are perfectly balanced by a handful of design-conscious hotels that allow visitors a respite from the city's chaos.

In recognition of Mexico City's growing appeal for a chic travel market, a mammoth renovation project is underway for the ancient heart of the city. The fruit of its labour is already visible in the city's immaculately sandblasted landmarks, such as the old Dirección General de Correos (General Post Office). Also part of this ever-changing cityscape are the wide, pristine pavements and state-of-the-art designer lampposts

PAGE 156: Colourful, flower-festooned trajineras (boats) cluster around the canals of Xochimilco.

THIS PAGE: The Angel of Independence towers over the capital's graceful boulevard, Paseo de la Reforma.

OPPOSITE: Mexico City's nightlife is legendary; here you can expect to dance till dawn.

along the main boulevard, Paseo de la Reforma, which was built in 1865 and modelled after the elegant Champs Élysées in Paris.

The project even includes visitor-friendly touches such as the policharros (police cowboys) on horseback. With their bolero jacket, trousers with glittery trimmings, and wide-brimmed sombrero (hat), the charro's (Mexican cowboy's) outfit—worn also by the mariachi (strolling musician)—has become something of a national costume. These policharros are all part of the city's visible efforts to guide and protect travellers to the historic zone, particularly around the much-visited Central Alameda area.

culture clash

Mexico City's name in Spanish is simply 'México' (pronounced as 'meh-hee-ko')—only rarely 'La Ciudad de México' (The City of Mexico) if the locals want to distinguish it from the rest of the country. Both city and country were named after the tribe of Mexica who settled in the Valley of Mexico in the early 14th century after extensive wandering.

The Mexicas and the Aztecs are, for most purposes, one and the same. Aztec is now used to refer to the dominant empire of the country, when the Spanish Conquest took place from 1519 to 1521.

Lured by tales of Aztec riches, Spanish conquistador Hernán Cortés journeyed from Cuba to the Gulf of Mexico. While bloody and rapacious, his march from the port of Veracruz in the east—between the two snow-capped volcanoes to Tenochtitlán, then a cluster of islands amid five rippling blue lakes—was apocryphal and an essential part of modern Mexico City's identity. It is possible to still feel the same sense of wonder and discovery that the Spanish must have felt on seeing the city for the first time.

In just two years, the Spanish invaded and destroyed the 3,000-year-old Aztec civilisation and their ancient capital of Tenochtitlán, founded around 1325. By the time the Spanish army arrived, it was already the largest city in the Western hemisphere. The early chroniclers testified that it was clean, orderly and breathtakingly beautiful. Using stones from the temples and palaces of Tenochtitlán, Cortés built the Plaza de la Constitución (Constitution Square), more commonly known as the zócalo or town square,

THIS PAGE (FROM TOP): The city is home to over 8 million people; mariachi waiting to enliven the many ongoing festivities.

OPPOSITE (FROM TOP): Policharros patrolling the streets on horseback; Spanish conquistadors as depicted in one of Diego Rivera's murals; the Palacio Nacional (National Palace).

that became the heart of Mexico City. Measuring more than 219 yd (200 m) on each side, it is one of the world's largest plazas, and the focus of the city's historic centre.

capital sights

A recommendation of Mexico City's highlights must begin with the Palacio Nacional (National Palace), where you can see the enormous murals of Mexico's best-known painter, Diego Rivera. Inside this elegant building on the east side of the zócalo, Rivera painted his idealised vision of Mexico's history from 1929 to 1945, and its struggle for independence. The rich spectacle depicts pre-Hispanic ceremonial centres, burial customs, textile dyeing and culinary traditions, all illustrated on the first floor—a teaser for the myriad sights in store.

Spread magnificently over the stairwell is Rivera's pro-socialist painting 'The Epic of the Mexican People in their Struggle for Freedom and Independence'. This is a perfect visual introduction to the country's past from the period of conquest up till the 1930s. In addition to the portrayal of world events and international figures—from the Inquisition to an image of Karl Marx—you may spot Rivera's wife and acclaimed painter, Frida Kahlo, to the left of the mural.

The couple's tumultuous relationship—Rivera's compulsive womanising and Frida's leg amputation, miscarriages and alcoholism, as well as their dedicated support of communism—is almost as famous as their art, in particular Rivera's paintings of rotund peasant women with braided hair and Frida's numerous self-portraits. Their relationship is the subject of *Frida*, a 2002 Hollywood film starring Mexican actress Salma Hayek.

From here, a visit to the Catedral Metropolitana (Metropolitan Cathedral) located on the northern side of the zócalo is imperative. Cortés purportedly uncovered over 136,000 skulls in its vicinity. Just east of the cathedral, past the drawing of drummers and dancers in loincloths and feathered headdresses, are the remains of the Templo Mayor (Great Temple) and its adjacent museum.

Accidentally unearthed in 1978, this was part of an archaeological site that was once the religious centre of the Aztec empire, offering a tragic example of how the Spaniards tore down former religious sites only to build their own churches on the exact same spots. The museum displays the artefacts discovered during the excavations.

sacred metropolis

The pyramids of Teotihuacán, the sacred metropolis of a mysterious pre-Aztec civilisation, are 31 miles (50 km) northeast of downtown Mexico. Despite the slight inconvenience of distance, many travellers to Mexico City make this visit their priority.

The towering Pirámide del Sol y de la Luna (Pyramids of the Sun and Moon) linked to the decorative Templo de Quetzalcóatl (Temple of the Plumed Serpent) by the 2-mile (3-km) Calzada de los Muertos (Avenue of the Dead), is one of the most spectacular and remarkable sites in Mexico.

These are one of the few major attractions open on Mondays, when nearly all of the country's museums, and most archaeological sites, are closed. There is no need to fret over transportation, as each of the hotels featured here will get you there and back. The site opens at 7 am, for those sensible enough to avoid the scorching heat of midday.

Visitors who don't fancy scaling 215-ft (65-m) pyramids in the blazing sun can visit the Museo Nacional de Antropología (National Museum of Anthropology). Designed by Mexican architect Pedro Ramírez Vásquez, the stunning pre-Columbian-style structure holds an extensive collection that sprawls across 11,111sq yd (9,290 sq m).

The collection comprises Mexico's major archaeological and ethnographical treasures, so you'll find all kinds of artefacts such as jewellery, pipes, spearheads and elaborate statues from some of world's greatest ancient civilisations, including the Olmecs and the Maya, on display.

From the amazing Aztec calendar stone called the Piedra del Sol, and the feathered coils of the plumed serpents, to Coatlicue, the notorious earth goddess with her skirt of snakes, the museum has more than most people can absorb in one visit.

THIS PAGE (FROM LEFT): The Museo
Nacional de Antropología houses
one of the finest archaeological
collections in the world;
the ancient hub of the Aztec
empire was the Templo Mayor,
dedicated to the god of
war, Huitzilopochtli.

OPPOSITE (FROM TOP): A conchero
dancer wearing a feathered
headdress drumming and
dancing in the zócalo;
the towering pyramids
of Teotihuacán.

THIS PAGE (FROM LEFT): *HABITA's floating glass cube concept has won T.E.N. Arquitectos many design awards; snatches of the streetscape through a clear strip of the sandblasted glass window.*

OPPOSITE (FROM TOP): *Coloured façades flank the streets of Mexico City; El Palacio de Bellas Artes (The Palace of Fine Arts) combines pre-Hispanic motifs with Art Deco architecture.*

building art

Besides its Aztec remains, exemplified by the Templo Mayor and Cuicuilco Pyramid in the south, Mexico City brims with Spanish colonial structures that embody the spirit of the Indian craftsmen who were used by the colonists as builders.

Their use of material, light, texture and careful conservation of space in the structures as well as their urge to hide images of pre-Hispanic gods and other divine creatures in the details are evident in these buildings.

Even as Mexico increasingly identifies with the West, its architectural approach to size, light and proportion, and emphasis on brilliant colours, contrasting tones and tactile surfaces remain distinct. As a design critic recently pointed out, Mexican architecture remains defined by the courtyard, the wall and an uninhibited use of colour, accompanied by a contemporary fascination with texture and monumental scale.

Modern architecture was born when the Mexican Revolution ended in the 1920s. It was propelled by technological advances utilising steel and reinforced concrete, along with the Revolution's call for a national expression through the arts. Luis Barragán (1902-1988), probably Mexico's most important contemporary architect, worked within a modernist framework, but incorporated his own sense of Mexican traditionalism with the use of thick walls, small openings, bright colours and natural materials. His vernacular creations, such as the Casa Antonio Galvez in San Ángel and the Casa Ortega in Tacubaya, have influenced the current generation of Mexican architects significantly.

Barragán's contemporary, Juan O'Gorman (1905-1982) produced the first functionalist structures, the most famous being the Casa Estudio de Diego Rivera in 1928, which is now a small musuem in San Ángel, and the National Autonomous University's library. The stars of contemporary Mexican architecture are Teodoro González de León, Abraham Zabludovsky, Ricardo Legoretta and Enrique Norton's group of T.E.N. (Taller Enrique Norton) Arquitectos. González de León and Zabludovsky are applauded for their talent in visualising pre-Columbian and colonial forms with 20th-century rationalism. Among their masterpieces is the Auditorio Nacional (National Auditorium) in Chapultepec Park in Mexico City.

Once you see HABITA, you will learn how to recognise T.E.N.'s signature glazed glass-covered buildings which are occupied by the hip offices and apartments of the Condesa. Other talented modernist architects to keep an eye on are Isaac Broid, who renovated the Centro de Imagen, a trendy photographic gallery you can visit in downtown Mexico City, and Mario Moreno Flores, responsible for the Centro Cultural X'Teresa (X'Teresa Cultural Centre) in the historic zone.

kahlo's coyoacán

The cobblestone streets of Coyoacán, 6 miles (10 km) south of the historic centre, is where Mexican painter Frida Kahlo, built her Blue House. This is one of the country's most intimate houses-turned-museums, filled with her sketchbooks, jewellery, ethnic dresses, easels and four-poster deathbed, as well as artworks by her contemporaries.

Down the road you can also visit the house of Kahlo's famous lover, Leon Trotsky, where his shattered glasses still testify to his brutal murder here in 1940.

Visitors to this enchanting part of town can shop for handicrafts in Coyoacán's central plazas on the weekends, or pop into the famous cantina (Western-style bar), La Guadalupana, for a shot of tequila with a sangrita—a thick, deep-red chaser made of tomato juice, orange juice, salt, a spritz of lime, and a splash of Tabasco sauce.

A popular contender for a day out is a leisurely boat ride along the floating gardens of Xochimilco. Visitors are served Mexican beers and soft drinks from ice-filled buckets, while local ladies in canoes dish out tortillas and quesadillas for sale from their simple waterborne grills.

Weekends are the liveliest when bands of floating mariachi (street musicians) join the throng. Xochimilco is a pleasant surprise for anyone who has only heard of the capital's traffic and ozone levels.

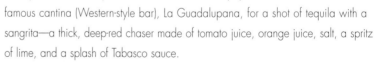

THIS PAGE (FROM LEFT): A vendor plies
the canals of Xochimilco
to sell her wares;
the name of each boat is spelt out
in cheery colours on the arches.

OPPOSITE (FROM TOP): Frida Kahlo's
Blue House is now a museum;
one of Kahlo's self-portraits
where she is captured in
traditional attire.

Inn in the south is Martini and margarita mecca. Fashionistas can be sighted at HABITA's rooftop Area bar and W hotel's sleek Whiskey Bar, while Rioma, Cinnabar and El Colmillo are *the* nightclubs of the Condesa. Mama Rumba, with its live salsa beats, sits on the edge of the Condesa, in Roma, where the popular Barracuda bar also resides.

The city's top art galleries have congregated in Polanco and Roma. The galleries of Alberto Misrachi, Oscar Roman and Juan Martín in Polanco, and the cultural centre of La Casa Lamm, Galería Nina Menocal and Galería ORM in Roma are mandatory stops for art aficionados. Mexico's most treasured modern art collection, however, is jealously guarded in the Museo de Arte Moderno, sandwiched between Roma and the Condesa.

In Polanco, Avenida Presidente Masaryk is lined with designer boutiques and stylish shops, and Zona Rosa (Pink Zone) is a fashionable shopping area with a concentration of chic New York-style boutiques and stores selling traditional Mexican souvenirs. The main thoroughfare of Paseo de la Reforma and the Liverpool department store also make fulfilling stops for shopaholics. In Roma, shops such as Chic by Accident, Ludens, Cooperative 244, Carmen Rión and El Palacio de Hierro may be found on the hoi-polloi hitlist, while Mob, Arte Faco and Kulte are the Condesa's trump cards.

Craft and souvenir markets selling ceramics, textiles, jewellery, leather and woodwork, include the Mercado La Lagunilla (Thieves' Market), El Bazar Sábado in San Ángel, and Mercado de la Ciudadela near the historic centre. On weekends, antique vendors from the Plaza del Ángel in the Zona Rosa set up a street market, and on Tuesdays, you can wander around the pretty Mercado de Ruedas (Market on Wheels) off Avenida Veracruz in the Condesa.

Avenida Michoacán is the place to go for grand Art Deco mansions from the 1930s and 40s. Soon the Condesa will have an eponymous hotel by the same hip group responsible for HABITA and Deseo [Hotel + Lounge] in Playa del Carmen, adding another gem to the city's skyline. This combination of architecture, culture and lively street scenes is what attracts many to Mexico City—its symbolic and natural abundance, its challenges to structure and definition, its chaos and sublimity. For many, here is the heart of the country, and the best place to start its exploration.

HABITA

THIS PAGE: *A brick fireplace keeps visitors warm at the rooftop bar.*

OPPOSITE (FROM TOP): *Opalescent glass walls separate Aura Restaurant from the streetscape; HABITA's interior is a measured interplay of inventive lighting and pockets of space; the hotel's sleek glacial structure offers guests a cool retreat.*

On its best of days, Mexico City can still be an assault on the senses—relentless traffic, smog and the unmistakable urban jangle of the most populous city in the country. Along one of the busiest streets in the Polanco district, however, rises a cool oasis. A member of Leading Hotels of the World since 2004, HABITA is a modern boutique hotel known as the city's 'ice cube'.

It certainly lives up to its name with its architecture—clean, minimalist and glass-veiled—providing a sudden and surprising shot of cool elegance in the hot city.

More specifically, HABITA is built like a cube within a cube. Behind its façade of translucent green-blue sandblasted glass, lies the concrete body of the building. The rooms open up to balconies that are

enclosed by glass acting as a protective sheath to insulate occupants from the noise and pollution of the street.

While this second 'skin' of the hotel plays a functional role in buffering guests from various urban maladies, its aesthetic effect is provocative and playful.

The hotel's 36 rooms and suites, spa and bar are veiled from outside view, while clear strips strategically inset into its frosted glass shell offer guests edited glimpses of the street scene made up of boulevards lined with trendy restaurants and luxury brand stores such as Emporio Armani, Fendi and Hugo Boss.

Its architecture is a paradox of shielding and revealing, denying and exposing. At night, when the hotel is illuminated between its 'skins', the building glows like a lantern, revealing just discernible shadows of fixtures and furnishings within.

The glass block belonged originally to a five-storey 1950s apartment building. The hotel's new 'box-within-a-box' concept becomes clear when you view the twin of the old building which sits derelict and vacant next to it.

The juxtaposition is most striking, and one realises how clever and skilful the architects have been in breathing new life into what was formerly a most squalid site despite the zoning restrictions and reconstruction rules imposed.

The building's façade may appear austere and almost aloof, but guests will be surprised at how thoughtfully hospitable, even cosy, its interior is. Pristine blond maple wood prevails, as do serene shades of white and ecru. Everything here is custom-made by TEN Arquitectos—tables, counters, the pigeonholes at the front desk and even the restaurant's ceramic tableware.

Care in details is evident in the sleek built-in furniture, stainless steel fittings and translucent glass partitions that are used to decorate the hotel. Insulated from the outside

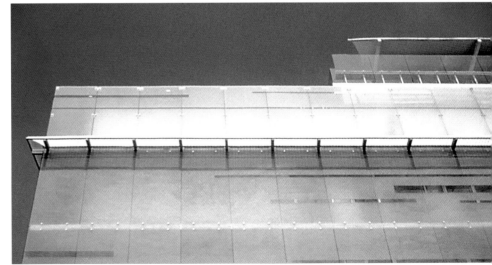

THIS PAGE (CLOCKWISE FROM RIGHT):
A ceramic mural provides the theatrical backdrop to the outdoor lap pool; creative concoctions are served in the restaurant's bar; clean lines, understated furnishing and natural light give the rooms a serene feel.
OPPOSITE: *The dazzling city skyline can be enjoyed from the hotel's rooftop bar and lounge.*

world, the general ambience is serene and inward focused, with generous pockets of calm, airy space. Outfitted with Eames chairs, Sony Vega flat-screen televisions, high-speed Internet access and Hermès bath toiletries, HABITA's rooms combine quality with technology and warm hospitality to create an intimate living area for the modern traveller.

In line with its minimalist approach and architectural theme of 'veiling', the hotel surprises its guests with a rather low-key check-in counter easily eclipsed by the hotel's dining room, Aura Restaurant. Blink and you might mistake it for the restaurant's reception. Redefining the concept of a hotel lobby, this is intentionally done to transform the entrance into a prime 'social zone'.

The city's chic gather to enjoy the inventive cuisine of chef Lula Martin del Campo at Aura, and the buzz at Area Bar

and Terrace upstairs. Area, an alfresco rooftop bar flanked by a lounge, a 12-ft- (4-m-) long open brick fireplace and a spiral staircase that leads down to a stunning lap pool and jacuzzi, offers guests unobstructed views of the city's skyline while they sip on the bar's stylish concoctions.

Since HABITA's reconstruction in 2000, Area has become the hottest venue for fashion shoots and shows, and a dramatic backdrop for night parties. With its white tiled walls and redwood deck, the outdoor lounge is the best setting for mingling with the hip and beautiful. And given the protective, almost cocoon-like structure of the hotel, this open-air celebration of the cityscape becomes all the more theatrical.

The HABITA experience is not complete without a visit to Aqua Spa, where guests can unwind in the sauna and outdoor whirlpool or by treating themselves to an exotic range of facial and body treatments. From reflexology and shiatsu to tuina and reiki, options on the spa menu seem endless. Visiting the solarium is an efficient alternative to baking in the blazing Mexican heat to perfect your tan. The 24-hour fitness centre offers a workout at any time of the day.

Like a glass box floating above Polanco, Mexico City's business and cultural centre, HABITA is a new style of lodging that defies convention, yet offers unparalleled service and comfort.

FACTS

ROOMS	32 rooms • 4 junior suites
FOOD	Aura Restaurant: inventive
DRINK	Area Bar and Terrace
FEATURES	Aqua Spa • heated pool • sauna • outdoor jacuzzi • solarium • garage • 24-hour fitness centre
BUSINESS	business centre • meeting room • personal assistant • high-speed Internet access
NEARBY	chic restaurants • designer shops • art galleries • museums
CONTACT	Avenida Presidente Masaryk 201, Colonia Polanco, Mexico City 11560 • telephone: +52.555 282 3100 • facsimile: +52.555 282 3101 • email: info@hotelhabita.com • website: www.hotelhabita.com

PHOTOGRAPHS BY JEAN-LUC LALOUX, COURTESY OF HABITA.

W Mexico City

THIS PAGE (CLOCKWISE FROM RIGHT):
Rooms exude warmth and
urban chic with red walls
and sensuous lighting;
bathrooms with hammocks and
window views double up
as lounge areas.
OPPOSITE: The stand-alone stone
tub is a signature feature of W's
stylish bathrooms.

From the time it was founded as the Aztec capital in 1325 to its capture by the Spanish crown, then to its triumph as an independent country, Mexico City had always been at the heart of all major political and cultural events in the country. Ranking as the largest city in the world, it buzzes with commercial activity by day, and by night, cosmopolitan bars and clubs maintain a non-stop tempo. It's only fitting then that the city, which is so impressively upbeat and has such a rich history, should play host to the first of the W hotels in Latin America.

Stylish yet functional, W hotels around the world are known for being witty and welcoming, and featuring the most spectacular modern architecture. Step in from the busy and fashionable Polanco neighbourhood into W Mexico City's all-glass entrance and be instantly 'cooled' by pools of clear water which guests seem to levitate over. This atmosphere of limitless clear space is immediately contrasted with a black lava stone tunnel leading to the reception area.

Aesthetically, the décor of the 25-storey hotel is astounding, even commanding,

Stylish yet functional, W hotels around the world are known for being witty and welcoming...

but everything serves a purpose to calm, cool and placate the senses from the city's frenetic pace. Indoor koi ponds provide meditative moments, while the images that flicker on the projection wall along guestroom corridors allow busy business travellers to stop in their tracks for a spot of quiet contemplation.

The hotel's 237 rooms are painted an audacious cherry red, to contrast strikingly with the all-white W signature beds with their famous white linen. But the star attraction must be the generously large bathrooms where rain showers for two are fitted with full-body water jets, and can even be turned into a lounging area with woven hammocks. And as with all W hotels, each room comes with an oversized work area and data connections, so guests can access the world as much or as little as they want.

The spa is outfitted with a juice bar and five modern treatment rooms that are encased by icy green glass. A touch of Mexican tradition can also be found in the Temazcal sauna. Gym regulars will find the glass-enclosed health club overlooking the street a good place to see and be seen.

Meal times are equally stylish at Solea restaurant, with its chocolate-coloured walls and ebony-stained floors, and the dramatic feature of a communal table at the entrance. Here, the hotel presents another architectural feat—a private dining room sunken several feet so that the lower half, enclosed by glass, will be visible to guests in the lobby.

For post-dinner drinks, visit The Whiskey, the exclusive and cosmopolitan outdoor terrace bar and lounge that offers an unbeatable view of Polanco with its rows of exclusive boutiques, art galleries and theatre. At W, guests can feel the pulse of the city resounding with its colourful history, and yet be blissfully cocooned within the stylish cool of the ultimate designer hotel.

FACTS

ROOMS	237 rooms
FOOD	Solea: Latin-Asian seafood
DRINK	The Whiskey • The Living Room
FEATURES	spa • Temazcal • large bathrooms with hammock in shower
BUSINESS	business centre • meeting facilities • conference centre • data ports in all rooms
NEARBY	Polanco • boutiques • restaurants • theatres • art galleries
CONTACT	Campos Eliseos 252, Colonia Polanco, Mexico City 11560 • telephone: +52.559 138 1800 • facsimile: +52.555 208 4090 • email: reservations.mexicocity@whotels.com • website: www.whotels.com

RADIO SERVICIO •MODELO• *tels.* 2-10

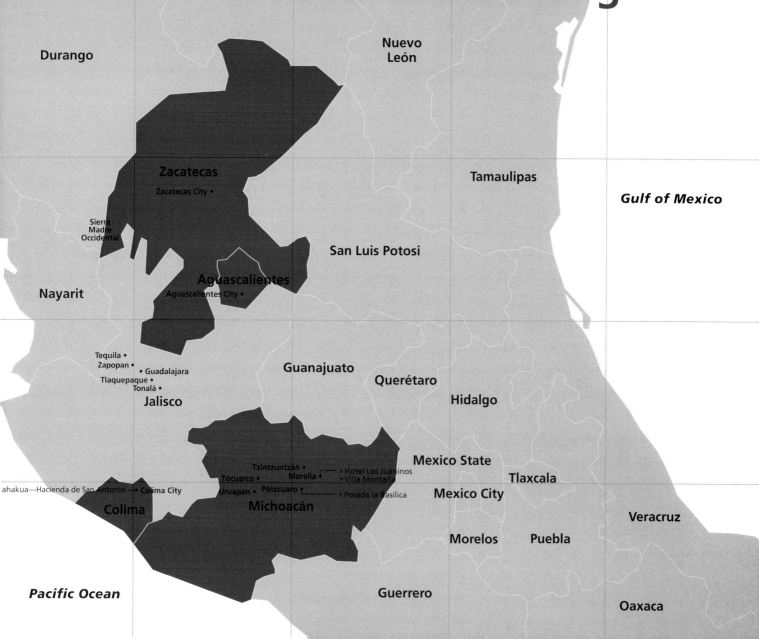

Chihuahua

Coahuila

centralwesternhighlands

Durango

Nuevo León

Zacatecas

Zacatecas City •

Tamaulipas

Gulf of Mexico

Sierra
Madre
Occidental

San Luis Potosi

Aguascalientes

Aguascalientes City •

Nayarit

Tequila •
Zapopan •
Tlaquepaque •
Tonalá •

• Guadalajara

Jalisco

Guanajuato

Querétaro

Hidalgo

Mexico State

Tzintzuntzán •
Tócuarco •
Morelia •
> Hotel Los Juaninos
> Villa Montaña

ahakua—Hacienda de San Antonio → Colima City

Uruapan • • Pátzcuaro

> Posada la Basílica

Tlaxcala

Mexico City

Colima

Michoacán

Morelos

Puebla

Veracruz

Pacific Ocean

Guerrero

Oaxaca

butterfly state

For those seeking an up-close, off-the-beaten-path encounter with nature, the extraordinarily diverse state of Michoacán will leave you awed by its remote blend of natural and cultural beauty. Undulating, green and dotted with lakes and valleys, much of its mountainous terrain and idyllic wildlife co-exist harmoniously with its indigenous inhabitants.

Life in this state moves along at its own pace. Architecturally, all three major cities of Morelia, Pátzcuaro and Uruapan remain largely unchanged from colonial times although they have been integrated into Mexico's commercial mainstream. Morelia, its well-preserved capital, was built by conquistadors in grand Spanish style, and hewn out of gorgeous pink stone. If Oaxaca is distinguished because of the greenish shade of its façades, Morelia is characterised by its enchanting pink hue.

Declared a World Heritage Site in 1991, Morelia is admired for its fine 18th-century colonial architecture, twin-towered cathedral (a combination of Herreresque, baroque and neoclassical styles), Michoacán State Museum, elaborate Clavijero Palace and the Fuente Las Tarascas (Tarascan Fountain) from which its famous aqueduct runs.

Almost everything of interest is within walking distance in Morelia. Less industrial and more elegant than Guadalajara, it is a visual treat, with beautiful arches and fountains adorning the streets. It is also a haunt for lovers of classical music, playing host to several annual music festivals, and a great place to learn Spanish with a number of language schools offering courses for foreign visitors.

Along the way be sure to pop by Casa de las Artesanías (House of Handicrafts), where folk art and handicrafts such as copperware, pottery and lacquerware from all over Michoacán are sold. Upstairs you'll find shops with artisans demonstrating how crafts from their hometowns are made. Handmade candies derived from traditional recipes are another of the town's specialities. Be sure to try them in any local shop.

A large indigenous population inhabits the villages around the scenic Lake Pátzcuaro, seemingly unaffected by modern trappings and retaining the distinct culture of its traditional dress, Purépecha language, music and dance. These villages produce many quality crafts including straw goods, clay sculptures, wood carvings and furniture,

PAGE 178: Introduced in the 16th century, bullfights are held on Sundays from October to March.

THIS PAGE (FROM TOP): The arches of El Aqueducto run for almost a mile (2 km) across the city of Morelia; Purépecha women can often be distinguished by their distinctive rebozo (shawl).

OPPOSITE: Buildings in Morelia are constructed in fine colonial style with arches, baroque façades and coloured stone walls.

ceramics, pottery and masks. Both the sights and sounds, combined with the friendliness of its people, provide a memorable experience for any visitor.

The picturesque town of Pátzcuaro is also synonymous with the Day of the Dead celebrations, held on November 1 and 2. Throngs of celebrants from all over Mexico descend here to catch the festivities taking place around the lake. During this religious festival, the Purépecha people honour the deceased with an all-night graveyard vigil, where altars are constructed and decorated with marigolds, candles, sweets, and skulls and skeletons made of sugar or papier-mâché. Families visit the tombs of their ancestors to offer food, drink and prayers. The festival culminates in a parade of decorated canoes, along with crafts markets, concerts and exhibitions held in the village square.

But it is the El Rosario Sanctuary that forms Michoacán's most memorable draw. This is the only place in the world where you can hear the hum of nearly 300 million butterflies fluttering together. From November to March, Michoacán's fir-forested mountains provide the breeding grounds for the migratory monarch butterfly. Each year these butterflies travel over 3,000 miles (4,828 km) from Canada and the northeastern part of the United States to reach their sanctuary in the central Mexican highlands. On sunny days, they fill the sky like brilliant, black-and-orange-coloured confetti.

tequila sunrise

The only thing more Mexican than tequila is the mariachi, and like its musical name Guadalajara, the capital of Jalisco state is known for its strolling street musicians. Indeed no image captures the spirit of Mexico better than that of the mariachi in matching silver-studded garb and wide-brimmed sombreros (hats), belting out Mexican ballads with violins, guitars and trumpets. Head for the Plaza de los Mariachis to get a memorable sampling of the music.

Those who appreciate this vibrant music should consider visiting when Guadalajara hosts an international mariachi festival in September. During this time, both traditional and modern mariachi music can be enjoyed at the many restaurants, bars and cafés lining the streets, on any night of the week.

THIS PAGE (FROM TOP): Monarch butterflies hibernate and breed for four months in sanctuaries; a Tarascan dance that dates back to pre-Hispanic times.
OPPOSITE: The austere grandeur of Morelia's cathedral is accentuated by its twin bell towers.

THIS PAGE: Guadalajara's Rotonda de los Hombres Ilustres is a monument to Jalisco's historic figures, six of whom are buried underneath it.

OPPOSITE (FROM TOP): The limestone columns of Teatro Degollado; the capital's cathedral contains 11 altars given by King Fernando VII of Spain.

This fun and lively city—Mexico's second largest—is also the birthplace of tequila, the sombrero, the charro (Mexican cowboy) and the Jarabe Tapatío (hat dance), and has managed to keep these icons alive without turning them into clichés. For a taste of Mexico's national drink, head 31 miles (50 km) northwest to the town of Tequila, where tequila is produced. All around, fields of blue agave from which tequila is distilled surround the town, filling the air with potent wafts of tequila. You can hop on the Tequila Bus or brave the Tequila Express for a raucous train ride to the various distilleries and agave fields. But if you prefer to stay in town, La Destilería has a tequila museum, restaurant and bar, where over 200 brands of tequila are sold.

This fun and lively city—Mexico's second largest—is also the birthplace of tequila...

As a prosperous agricultural region and departure point for Spanish expeditions, Guadalajara rapidly grew to become one of colonial Mexico's most important cities. Mexico's independence leader, Miguel Hidalgo, set up a short-lived revolutionary government here in 1810, but was executed soon after his capture in 1811. Muralist José Clemente Orozco's powerful 1937 portrait of the revolutionary—Hidalgo brandishing a torch high in his fist, with the crowd at his feet—may be found in the Palacio de Gobierno (Government Palace). Upstairs in the Congress Hall, another mural by Orozco depicts Hidalgo and other monumental figures of Mexican history.

Nearby, the city's twin-towered cathedral, constructed in 1558, is a melange of baroque and gothic styles, containing some of the world's most beautiful altars and a priceless 17th-century painting of La Asunción de la Virgen (The Assumption of the Virgin) by Bartolomé Murillo. You can walk from here to the gilded, neoclassical Teatro Degollado, which the Jalisco Philharmonic Orchestra calls home.

Behind the theatre lies Plaza Tapatía, the city's focal point and historic centre lined with shops, restaurants, fountains and sculptures, leading to the grand landmark of Instituto Cultural Cabañas at the end. Originally an orphanage and hospice for over 150 years, this cultural gem now hosts some spectacular art exhibitions. Orozco's finest murals, including the poignant El Hombre de Fuego (Man of Fire), grace the main chapel's dome. There are 53 other frescoes that line the walls and ceilings of the chapel, while the museum features over 100 paintings and drawings by Orozco.

With Tlaquepaque (pronounced as 'la-keh-pah-keh') less than 4 miles (7 km) southeast of the city, and the cobblestone streets of Tonalá or Lake Chapala nearby, there are enough attractions to keep visitors to Guadalajara busy for at least five days. Tlaquepaque has stylish restaurants and galleries converted from old country homes, and its upscale shops are filled with bronze sculptures, ceramics, glassware and embroidered clothing from all over Mexico.

On Thursdays and Sundays, the town of Tonalá is transformed into a massive street market with crafts at great bargains, where you can spend a day to explore. But if you're looking for collectible pieces, head for its glassware and ceramic factories.

nature's nest

Mexico's Central Western Highlands offer diverse climates and lush countryside stretching from the southern points of the Sierra Madre Occidental in the north of Jalisco, to the western edges of the Sierra Madre del Sur, behind the Pacific coast. This area is marked with a rich topography of mountain ranges, green plains, warm coasts, abundant rivers and lakes.

Michoacán's natural attractions include the crystalline lake of Zirahuén and the village of Santa Clara del Cobre, famed for its copperware. The town of Tupataro, sought after for its intricate hand-carved woodwork and 16th-century church with intricately painted ceilings, should also be listed on your itinerary.

The state's significant stretch of tropical Pacific coastline is relatively undeveloped, providing strong waves for surfing. Its landscape is one of the most rugged in Mexico, and its territory is marked by great elevations and profound depressions. Inland, the climate is temperate, so visitors to Pátzcuaro should be prepared for a cool winter and rainy summer, while Morelia is much warmer and can really heat up around midday.

Visitors are often surprised to find this part of Mexico, overflowing with nature, teeming with forests, mountains, extinct volcanoes and wild flowers. For those looking for an adrenaline rush, Guadalajara is a paradise for rock climbers and the granite boulders of El Diente (The Tooth) in Zapopan is a good place to start. This mountain got its name from its teeth-like rocks, which call for some very imaginative manoeuvres. A meeting place for all rock climbers, this is where the sport first began in Guadalajara.

More advanced climbers can try scaling La Hidro, close to the village of Mesa Colorada. Made of basalt, the rock can be rough on the hands, but fantastic views of the ravine make up for it. The same is true of El Cuajo, another excellent spot for climbing located in the Huaxtla canyon. The beautiful rock is formed by basalt walls about 263 ft (80 m) high and surrounded by lush tropical vegetation.

Another place that testifies to the power of nature in these highlands is the Volcán Paricutín, a short distance from the town of Uruapan. This volcano rose out of farmland

THIS PAGE (CLOCKWISE FROM TOP):
The Antiguo Colegio de Pátzcuaro, an old Jesuit school in Pátzcuaro; copper pots and plates fashioned in Santa Clara del Cobre; Zirahuén's panoramic lake with forests lining its shores.
OPPOSITE: *A shop in Santa Clara del Cobre sells wooden masks, clay sculptures and skeletons for Day of the Dead celebrations.*

in 1943, reaching 1,345 ft (410 m) above the surrounding land in less than a year and emitting lava until 1952. Now you can visit the volcanic cone in complete safety and spot the ruins of San Juan Church protruding from the sea of solidified black lava. To ascend the volcano you can ride a horse to the base and climb the summit, or walk the trails with the help of a guide.

waterland

Far from Mexico's major pre-Hispanic empires, Michoacán stems from an agricultural society with its main ethnic and linguistic group developing in the northern areas between the 14th and 16th centuries. The Aztecs, who never conquered them, called them Michoaques and their land Michoacán, which means 'the place where fish are abundant' because it was once an extensive network of lakes. Chroniclers of early colonial days called them Tarascans, but today they are known as Purépecha.

The heart of the Tarascan empire was the ancient capital of Tzintzuntzán (Place of the Hummingbirds), about 10 miles (16 km) northeast of Pátzcuaro. Here you can climb up the hill to the five temples of Las Yacatas, which overlooks the town and lake of Pátzcuaro. Apart from its unusual, key-shaped pyramids known as yácatas, Tzintzuntzán (pronounced as 'seen-soon-sahn') is also noted for its 16th-century Franciscan monastery—the Ex-Convento de San Francisco embellished with Moorish ceilings, coffered archways, winged angels, frescoes and a painted relief of the Entombment of Christ. The monastery is fronted by an atrium of olive trees said to be the oldest in the Americas, brought here from Spain by the Franciscan monks.

The people of Michoacán succumbed to the invasion of the Spaniards in the 1520s and faced cruel persecution by Nuño de Guzmán, one of the most ruthless figures in the Conquest, who arrived in 1529 in his quest for gold. Further decline in the Tarascan population was prevented by the arrival of Vasco de Quiroga in 1533. Pátzcuaro's main plaza and exciting market town of Quiroga was named after this charismatic evangelist who left an indelible mark on the town.

Vasco de Quiroga began his humanitarian mission by grouping the indigenous people into specialist communities and training them in different disciplines and trades. The results can still be seen in the lakeside villages, where Santa Clara is known for its copperware, Nurío for hand-woven wool products, Paracho for guitars, Tzintzuntzán for pottery, Zirahuén for knives and Tócuaro for hand-carved masks. The skills he imparted to the Tarascans of Pátzcuaro have been passed down to their descendents, who are among the best master craftsmen in Mexico.

When he was appointed bishop, Vasco de Quiroga built one of Mexico's first hospitals on what is now the site of Casa de los Once Patios (House of 11 Courtyards), a short walk from Plaza Vasco de Quiroga. Today the house hosts small artisan shops specialising in regional crafts. Shoppers will find a handsome selection of gold-leafed lacquerware, hand-painted ceramics and textiles.

Built atop the hill of a pre-Hispanic ceremonial site, Vasco de Quiroga's tomb lies inside the Basílica de Nuestra Señora de la Salud (Basílica of Our Lady of Health), whose revered statue of the Virgin (made from corn cob and honey paste) attracts pilgrims all year round. This statue was made by the Tarascans upon Quiroga's request and the church was intended to be the centrepiece of his Michoacán community.

Soon worshippers began to experience miraculous healings and Quiroga had the words 'Salus Infirmorum' (Healer of the Sick) inscribed at the Virgin's feet. Ever since, pilgrims from all over the country have come here to ask the Virgin for help, making their way on their knees across the plaza and into the church through its passageways.

When exploring nearby villages and savouring the markets of the Michoacán region, many visitors will rent a car or take a tour, but if you don't mind taking a bus like the locals, this is a part of the country where the streets and public transport are safe, and probably one of the reasons why it is so close to the hearts of those acquainted with it.

street cuisine

More cultures thrive in the state of Michoacán than in any other part of the Central Western Highlands, and the breadth and depth of cuisine styles mirror the area's rich history and resources. Each community has its own interpretation of regional stews, pastries and huchepos (sweet corn tamales), and all are appropriate fare for the climate.

Michoacán is prized for its sopa tarasca—tomato-based bean soup with cream, cheese, dried chilli and bits of crisp tortilla. The state is also known for the tart, piquant flavours of dishes like salpicon de res (shredded beef cooked with pickled serranos, cilantro and tomatoes), and game such as rabbit and quail for the more adventurous palates.

You can get the famous pescado blanco (translucent, milky-coloured fish) from the fish stands around the jetty of Lake Pátzcuaro, or a cup of charales (tiny fish resembling whitebait, fried in batter and garnished with lime and chilli powder) for a snack. The market on the corner of Plaza Gertrudis Bocanegra is a good place to start savouring Pátzcuaro's treats. But if you prefer a more elegant setting, Restaurant Doña Paca offers churipo, a regional beef-and-vegetable stew served with corundas (triangular tamales).

In Morelia, the candy capital of Mexico, traditional sweets are very much part of the scene. It has a market and dulcerías just for sweets, and some of the most popular are dulces morelianos (made of milk and sugar), ate (jellied fruit) and cajeta (caramelised goat milk). You can even learn how these sweets and those from other parts of the state are made at the Sweets Museum along Avenida Madero.

Wash it all down with a traditional beverage, charanda, which is brandy made of sugar cane. It doesn't make much of an impression when taken on its own, but mix it with fruit punch, and you'll have a most tantalising cocktail. Like its cuisine, you will find endless surprises in Michoacán—from a variety of climates, provincial towns, bustling cities, and traditions that delight the senses with aromas and tastes, to the scenery which makes for a completely unforgettable trip.

THIS PAGE: *Traditional fare from the street stalls of Pátzcuaro.*

OPPOSITE (FROM TOP): *Ceramic plates and crafts displayed in a Michoacán shop; the regional specialities of Posada la Basílica in Michoacán.*

Hotel Los Juaninos

It's hard to find a more prestigious hotel than Los Juaninos. Formerly the Episcopal Palace, the magnificent grounds have now been converted into a hotel so luxurious it even exceeds the five-star category. Embellished with the fanciful French décor of the 18th century, with neoclassical and gothic touches, this mansion was considered too ostentatious for the residence of the town bishop for whom it was originally designed, and was eventually given up for secular use. The building was then converted into a hotel at the end of the 19th century, supported by the patronage of wealthy visitors who came to the town of Morelia via the newly opened Mexico City-Morelia railway line.

After undergoing a massive restoration exercise in 1998, the former palace reopened as Hotel Los Juaninos—the grandest hotel in Morelia, and a designated

THIS PAGE (CLOCKWISE FROM TOP):
Guests can ascend the majestic staircase lit by the skylight; interiors are marked by arched windows and classic furniture; imbued with nostalgia, rooms are a blend of past and present.

OPPOSITE: La Azotea on the rooftop is fronted by princely views of the grand cathedral.

heritage site for the pink-stone city. Upon arrival, vistors are led on a journey through its glamorous past, passing stately corridors of the French era, bold staircases of Spanish design, and intricate stained windows of the Art Nouveau period. Included throughout are subtle touches of indigenous Mexican culture in the tapestries, carpets and colourful tiles that blend artfully with the European décor.

Adding an invigorating slice of the contemporary is the steel-and-glass elevator which ferries guests from the lobby to the second floor. Standing out amidst its plush surroundings, the modern elevator contributes a surprising dash of the avant-garde to the historical setting.

Guests continue to discover Los Juaninos' surprises in its 30 guestrooms, set around two courtyards. It could be the original woodwork that has been finely restored, wood-panelled bathrooms,

elaborate arches or European-style bathtubs. All rooms are palatial and stately, each distinctly furnished with antique carpets and enormous beds. Step out onto the balconies and guests can enjoy an unobstructed vista of the city, and for some, the imposing cathedral which the hotel faces.

Fitting with the sumptuous lifestyle Los Juaninos affords, meals here are truly sublime affairs with the haute Mexican cuisine of La Azotea, the hotel's rooftop restaurant. Not to be missed are the delicate combinations of egg-coated pot cheese filled with pumpkin flowers in poblano chilli sauce, and the smoked trout in creamy macadamia nut sauce.

After dinner, head for the Rincon de Los Remedios bar which offers 'remedies' in the form of 'chinguirrín' and 'juaninos' cocktails. They could certainly help ease the feeling of regret when guests finally leave Los Juaninos' posh, pampering grounds.

FACTS

ROOMS	20 superior rooms • 7 junior suites • 3 master suites
FOOD	La Azotea: haute Mexican
DRINK	Rincon de Los Remedios
FEATURES	neoclassical, gothic and art nouveau décor • access to golf course and spa • guided tours upon request
BUSINESS	business centre • meeting room • Internet access • secretarial services
NEARBY	cathedral • shops • plazas
CONTACT	Morelos Sur 39, Centro Histórico, Morelia, Michoacán 58000 • telephone: +52.443 312 0036 • facsimile: +52.443 312 0036 • email:reservaciones@hoteljuaninos.com.mx • website: www.hoteljuaninos.com.mx

Posada la Basílica

If you're searching for a quieter Mexico, a slower paced paradise with all the colour and seductions of the country but without the frenzied tourism and heady nightlife, come to Pátzcuaro. The serene town, hidden away on a sunny hillside by a lake 240 miles (386 km) from Mexico City, seems worlds away from all that is urban.

Though the colonial town may now be a sleepy nook in the state of Michoacán, it was once a seat of power ruled by Bishop Don Vasco de Quiroga. He continues to live on in the numerous plazas, squares, streets and institutions named after him, and was instrumental in developing the local arts of the area. For that reason, the town is a haven for shoppers hoping to

bring home an authentic piece of Mexico with them. A string of craft villages surrounds Lake Pátzcuaro, each with its own speciality, from ceramics to tapestry and lacquerwork.

A hive of artisan activity, it's difficult to explore the town without coming across streets of vendors hawking their wares. The pace is unhurried and the mood relaxed—visitors can stroll through the shaded plazas and markets, admire the many well-preserved colonial buildings, or climb atop the hill of the Basílica, overlooking Calle Buena Vista. During the 55-mile (89-km) tour of the lake, visitors can certainly get their dose of retail and scenic therapy.

Within this sedentary setting is Posada la Basílica, an intimate 12-room hotel facing

THIS PAGE (FROM TOP): A cosy nook for tea on the balcony; perched on a hill, the hotel overlooks the cobbled streets and red-tiled roofs.

OPPOSITE (FROM LEFT): Rooms are infinitely cosy with fireplaces, murals and crisp sheets; Mexican meals and views of the town may be enjoyed from Tekare's dining room.

...warm colours correspond with wooden floors, local handicrafts and antique furniture.

Meals are had in Tekare, which also offers alfresco dining in the courtyard. In the evenings, diners sit round a blazing fire outdoors, while classic Mexican cuisine is served up in traditional black earthenware. Head for the restaurant's bar after dinner and ask for its speciality—margarita with freshly squeezed blackberry juice. Then enjoy your drink at your own pace as you admire the lake and hills beyond. If you're looking for a slower Mexico, you've come to a part of it where time almost stands still.

a lush stretch of gardens. Formerly an 18th-century retreat of a nobleman, the property was converted into a small hotel in the 1940s. Losing none of its tranquillity with its dramatic transformation, Posada la Basílica remains quaint, quiet and cosy, with many rooms offering views of the town, mountains and lake. Providing a warm respite from the cool weather are the fireplaces in some rooms, while the floor-to-ceiling window shutters allow the mild sun to stream in. Spacious and cheerful, warm colours correspond with wooden floors, local handicrafts and antique furniture.

FACTS

ROOMS	12 rooms
FOOD	Tekare: Mexican
DRINK	Tekare
FEATURES	fireplaces in some rooms
BUSINESS	meeting room
NEARBY	Lake Pátzcuaro • gardens of Basílica of Our Lady of Health • 17th-century Templo del Sagrario • plazas
CONTACT	6 Arciga, Pátzcuaro, Michoacán 61600 • telephone: +1.800.288 4282 (US) or +52.434 342 1108 • facsimile: +52.434 342 0659 • email: hotelpb@hotmail.com • website: www.posadalabasilica.com

PHOTOGRAPHS BY ERWAN FICHOU, COURTESY OF POSADA LA BASÍLICA.

Villa Montaña

First-time visitors to Mexico might think the whole country is a never-ending strip of white sand separated by the occasional stretch of cactus-filled desert. Venture inward, however, and they'll discover there is so much more to this sprawling land than sun, surf and margaritas.

The middle of Mexico is especially riveting. Seemingly created for the adventure traveller, it is filled with Indian motifs and countless pre-historic sites. Then there are the Spanish-influenced towns that are so rich in colonial splendour, they'll satiate even the most ardent Europhile with their beautifully restored European architecture.

Morelia, the capital of Michoacán, is a particularly outstanding colonial beauty. Renowned as a centre of arts and crafts, the peaceful town attracts writers, artists, philosophers and poets who make it their home. Restful and clean, Morelia provides a fresh respite from Mexico's sultry shores with its perennially cool weather, wide boulevards, lovely squares and shady parks. There are numerous masterfully restored mansions, churches and buildings with delicate façades, many of which are crafted out of pink-coloured stone.

Next to art and architecture, the other big attraction in Morelia is the opportunity to stay at Villa Montaña—a grand hotel perched high on a hill, overlooking the pretty salmon-coloured city below.

There is nothing rustic or rough about Villa Montaña. Surrounded by acres of blooming gardens filled with antique stone statues, rooms and suites are large and impressively furnished with tiled floors, a seating area and fireplace. French owner Philippe de Reiset, has taken great pains to create an effect of utmost elegance by styling each room individually with colonial antiques, carpets and Michoacán handicrafts. His attention to detail is quite exquisite.

THIS PAGE (CLOCKWISE FROM TOP):
The lobby is decorated with the owner's art and antique collection; the patio by the pool commands a magical view of the scenery; the restaurant attracts diners with its skilful blend of European favourites with regional tastes.

OPPOSITE: Guest cottages are tiered to offer panoramic views from their terraces or balconies.

The hotel grounds, embellished with multi-coloured flowers, towering fir trees and ivy-covered stone walls, are also a delight in themselves, and guests can admire the artful landscaping from their private terraces.

Villa Montaña remains busy throughout the year. In winter, it offers an indulgent abode with fireside cosiness, and in summer, its altitude and fresh breezes make it a cool retreat from the sunny beaches.

Besides, the area offers lots of attractions for all seasons: warmer months are filled with festivals, and in winter, there's the much-anticipated annual monarch butterfly migration to the El Rosario Sanctuary, a two-hour drive away.

And whatever the weather, the surrounding area, from the green waters of Lake Pátzcuaro, to the rolling hills, winding rivers and green valleys, is a pleasure to explore. Staying at the exquisite Villa Montaña just completes the perfection.

FACTS		
ROOMS	36 rooms and suites
FOOD	Villa Montaña Restaurant: international and regional
DRINK	Bar Terraza
FEATURES	fireplaces in all rooms • heated pool • fitness centre • spa • tennis court • boutique
BUSINESS	meeting and banquet rooms • business centre • audio-visual equipment • Internet access
NEARBY	golf course • horseback riding • historic centre of Morelia • excursions to craft towns
CONTACT	Patzimba 201, Colonia Vista Bella, Morelia, Michoacán 58090 • telephone: +52.443 314 0231 • facsimile: +52.443 315 1423 • email: reservaciones@villamontana.com.mx • website: www.villamontana.com.mx

PHOTOGRAPHS OF POOL AND COURTYARD BY ERWAN FICHOU. ALL PHOTOGRAPHS COURTESY OF VILLA MONTAÑA.

Mahakua—Hacienda de San Antonio

There are holidays that are filled with afternoon teas, shopping and massages—enjoyable but forgettable. And then there are those at Mahakua—Hacienda de San Antonio in Western Mexico, where days are spent horseback riding through the mountains, spotting deers, chipmunks and muskrats that populate the grounds, or simply lazing around the beautifully tiled pool. The gardens are lush and green, and the view dominated by two volcanoes.

This luxurious experience of living in a real Mexican estate would go down especially well with discerning travellers since the Hacienda is managed by the very posh Amanresorts, and run by the group's subsidiary, Maha. Being the first venture into Mexico for Amanresorts, a hotel brand that has successfully carved its own niche for luxurious hospitality, the Hacienda certainly lives up to its five-star standards with incomparable taste and elegance.

The resort, about a two-and-a-half-hour drive from Guadalajara, is sprawled across 470 acres (190 hectares) of grounds set within a massive 5,000-acre

(2,023-hectare) working ranch, dairy farm and coffee plantation, and centres on a 19th-century hacienda that still retains the roominess and classic feel of a traditional casa grande.

The two-storey compound contains 25 generously-sized suites, each individually decorated with Latin-American art, ancient textiles, hand-woven rugs and murals. Evidence of the Hacienda's surroundings can be spotted in volcanic stone features such as the winding staircase, traditional fireplaces and arches.

However, unlike the awe-inspiring architecture of the other Aman properties, the Hacienda's approach is deliberately homely. You're welcome to step into the casa's open kitchen with your pick of produce from the Hacienda's organic farm, and whip up a snack for yourself. Otherwise, you could leave it to the more-than-capable hands of the Hacienda's

chefs and choose to dine in the candlelit dining room, outdoor patio, poolside pavilion or second-floor terrace.

It is very much a self-contained setup, with the ranch producing dark Arabica coffee, fruit, vegetables, cheese, milk and honey. The organic farm includes roaming cows, pigs, chickens, goats and llamas.

And there's even more on the Hacienda's grounds. You can stroll through the courtyards decorated with brightly-hued flowers and graced with stones and columns; admire the workings of an arched aqueduct built from volcanic stone in 1904; or have a quiet moment in the chapel of San Antonio which is linked to the main house and still in use for local village festivals.

With abundant flora and fauna, as well as the homeliest hacienda, who says a farm stay in Mexico can't be a highly elegant and luxurious affair?

PHOTOGRAPHS COURTESY OF AMANRESORTS.

FACTS		
	ROOMS	22 suites • 3 grand suites
	FOOD	meals prepared with organic produce from the Hacienda's farm are served in the grand dining room, outdoor patio, poolside pavilion or terrace
	FEATURES	working ranch • organic farm • coffee plantation • view of 2 volcanoes • pool • tennis court • amphitheater • corral • library
	NEARBY	historical town of Colima • Manzanillo city for marlin and sailfishing • old town of Tlaquepaque in Guadalajara for shopping
	CONTACT	Municipio de Comala, Colima 28450 • telephone: +52.312 313 4411 • facsimile: +52.312 314 3727 • email: hacienda@mahakua.com.mx or reservations@amanresorts.com • website: www.amanresorts.com

seaofcortez

Tijuana
Mexicali
Ensenada
Reserva de la Biósfera
El Pinacate y Gran
Desierto de Altar
Puerto Penasco

Baja California Norte

Sonora

Bahía de
los Ángeles
Hermosillo
Bahía Kino

Sea
of
Cortez

Chihuahua

San Carlos
Guaymas

Bahía Magdalena

Santa Rosalía

> Hacienda de Los Santos — Álamos

Baja California Sur

Sinaloa

Lorento

Pacific Ocean

Durango

La Paz

Todos Santos — > Hotel California

San José del Cabo — > Casa Natalia
> Westin Regina Los Cabos
> Marquis Los Cabos
Cabo San Lucas — > Las Ventanas al Paraíso

stretch for the jet set

The Sea of Cortez (also known as the Gulf of California), with its tranquil blue waters, stretches of saguaro cacti, ancient cave paintings, quaint mission towns and isolated fishing villages, offers travellers a picture-perfect version of Mexico as the world imagines it. Situated in the northwestern reaches of the country, it divides the 1,000-mile (1,609 km) Peninsula of Baja California from the states of Sonora and Sinaloa.

Long considered an adventure destination, the Baja Peninsula has been drawing visitors, especially those from the United States, since the transpeninsular highway was completed in 1973. Interestingly, Los Cabos (The Capes) at the southernmost tip, used to be accessible only by yacht or private plane and only made it onto the map in the 1980s. The Los Cabos Corridor, a 20-mile (32-km) stretch of coastline connecting the towns of San José del Cabo and Cabo San Lucas, has not lost its privileged appeal. Its glamorous hotels and championship golf courses make it a top choice for the jet set.

For fishing, sailing and scuba diving enthusiasts, the Sea of Cortez will fulfil even the wildest marine dreams. French oceanographer Jacques Cousteau once described it as 'the world's greatest natural aquarium' because of its high content of phytoplankton, which sustains an astounding variety of life. This resource makes the region as unique for Mexico as the Galapagos Islands are for Ecuador.

In Loreto, you can expect to catch dorado, marlin and sailfish in summer, and cabrillo and snapper all year round. Scuba divers can commune with playful sea lions, whales, giant manta rays, hammerhead sharks, elephant seals and sea turtles as they cavort in the sea. Surfers say waves in Punto Perfecto rival those of Hawaii, while other hot spots for surfing are Playa Acapulguitos, Playa Monumentos and Costa Azul in Los Cabos.

Brimming with all kinds of activities, the region is host to major events such as fishing tournaments held in Cabo San Lucas in October and November, the annual Cabo Jazz Festival at the end of July, and the pre-Lenten Carnival or Mardi Gras (which usually takes place between mid- and late February) in San Felipe and La Paz on the gulf coast. On June 1, the Día de la Marina Nacional (National Navy Day) is a cheerful spectacle, as is the Fiesta de la Vendimia (Wine Harvest), celebrated in

PAGE 200: The Sea of Cortez is where desert meets tropical sea.

THIS PAGE: There are 136 species of agave in North America.

OPPOSITE: Baja's vegetation is scattered with giant cacti, yucca and desert shrubs.

mid-August in Ensenada, the heart of Baja wine country. Those who like to be on the move can try diving and windsurfing, while inland, canyoning, fossil hunts, rock climbing and cave painting tours provide exhilarating challenges.

Since the early 1980s, world-class golf courses, spas and high-end resorts have flourished with the development of the Los Cabos Corridor. Long before you arrive, you'll recognise this destination by its slender landmark—El Arco (The Arch)—a natural gateway sculpted out of rocky cliff by the Pacific Ocean at the foot of the cape. An icon synonymous with this luxury holiday hub, Los Cabos is said to receive an average of 360 days of sunshine a year.

Just off the coast about 50 miles (80 km) north of Cabo San Lucas is Todos Santos, where Mexican crafts feature prominently alongside this pretty colonial town popular with artists and art lovers. Host to an arts festival in late January and a tour of historic homes in February, Todos Santos provides a pleasing provincial alternative to the commercial feel of Cabo San Lucas.

THIS PAGE: The Sonoran Desert occupies both sides of the Sea of Cortez and most of Baja California.

OPPOSITE (FROM TOP): A Mexican cowboy in Sonora; the desert landscape is abundant with cacti such as sahuaro, cardon and organ pipe.

Sonora is pretty much cowboy country, but travellers tend to set their sights on the state's beaches in the coastal towns of Puerto Peñasco, Bahía Kino and Puerto San Carlos. Fishing, scuba diving, surfing, kayaking and yacht cruises are popular activities. Los Álamos is another beautifully restored colonial town in the state, with a baroque-style church built in the mid-18th century and timeless cobblestone streets.

cactus country

At its narrowest point, the Baja Peninsula—often referred to simply as Baja—is only 13 miles (21 km) wide, so you can easily have breakfast on one coast, cross the mountains and have lunch on the other. At its widest, it is 120 miles (193 km) of stunning desert, sea and mountains so rich in minerals that the rocks gleam red, gold and bluish green, making it one of the world's most biologically diverse regions.

Besides being one of earth's richest areas for cactus, the area is also home to the rare and enormous Humboldt squid, which ranges in size from 10 to 49 ft (3 to 15 m). Fishing here is strictly controlled and a new project committed to preserving the region's ecological treasures is underway.

Baja comprises two states—Baja California Norte (or Baja Norte) which begins at the Mexican-American border with Tijuana-San Diego on the California coast; and Baja California Sur (or Baja Sur), 440 miles (710 km) south. By far the most populated region is Baja Norte, where the daring can brave the 'sin city' of Tijuana, a fast-growing metropolis of casinos and cabarets, with a population of over 2 million.

The region includes other border towns such as Mexicali and the beer-producing Tecate, while Ensenada, 65 miles (104 km) south of the Pacific coast, marks the beginning of Mexico's wine country. The wineries in Ensenada's 'Bordeaux belt' of sheltered valleys produce almost 90 per cent of Mexico's wines, the best of which are produced in Valle de Guadalupe, Valle de Santo Tomás, and Valle de San Vicente. The scenery itself—picturesque vineyards surrounded by mountains—certainly merits a trip.

Much of Baja Sur's remote terrain remains rugged and desolate. Dusty, unpaved roads zigzag through the mountainous sierra, linking outposts of crumbling adobe shacks

with secluded towns that still bear the imprint of Spanish missionaries. Santa Rosalía, for example, was built on the Sea of Cortez by a French copper mining company in the mid-1800s. It is redolent of bygone days with its timber-framed façades, sloped roofs, and prefabricated church designed by Gustave Eiffel, who gave Paris the Eiffel Tower.

Baja Sur's capital and major port is La Paz (Peace), dubbed the City of Pearls. This peaceful, waterfront city is a paradise with hot deserts and cool oceans in different shades of blue and green. Blessed with clear calm waters, sunny weather and flawless beaches such as La Concha, water sports remain a highlight of the area.

You can also catch music, dance and theatre performances at the city's cultural centre, Teatro de la Ciudad, while the Museo Regional de Antropología e Historia (Regional Anthropology and History Museum) provides information on the Peninsula's history and people. The museum features recreations of the Comondu and Las Palmas Indian villages as well as Mexican cave paintings.

La Paz is the ferry port to Mazatlán and has its own mini peninsula with the port of Pichilingue, formerly known for its black pearl industry, but now an excellent place for ostiones diablo—raw oysters doused in a hot chilli sauce. South of La Paz, the town of Los Barriles is Baja's windsurfing capital with its powerful westerly winds and thundering waves. This makes it a regular venue for international competitions.

For those used to the sights and sounds of mainland Mexico, particularly in the south of the country where more typical cultures thrive, this region—from its language to the ethnic groups that inhabit it—is unfamiliar territory.

Baja cuisine is excellent and often surprisingly straightforward, and you are more likely to come across grilled steak and seafood than the more challenging and complicated concoctions that beckon in the southeast.

cape crosby

Cabo is the Spanish word for 'cape', and indeed, this starkly beautiful area at the southern point of the Peninsula is so relaxing and indulgent, it is said to be Baja California's equivalent of the Riviera Maya. In addition to sailing, surfing, windsurfing

THIS PAGE: *Baja's speciality is fresh seafood.*
OPPOSITE: *Glistening rock formations stand guard over the sand dunes of Los Cabos.*

and whale-watching, its breathtaking championship golf courses are suited to golfers of every skill level—the 27-hole Palmilla Golf Club, the18-hole El Dorado Golf Course and Cabo del Sol Ocean Course, all three designed by Jack Nicklaus.

With its dramatic seascape, craggy cliffs and rocks cradled by a spectacular marine environment, Los Cabos is the ultimate retreat where visitors can truly relinquish all urban stress. This is the heart of Mexico's thriving spa scene.

Today San José del Cabo, a charming 18th-century Jesuit mission town lying 115 miles (180 km) south of La Paz and Cabo San Lucas, is the Peninsula's prime tourist destination. Rumour has it that in the days when you could only reach the cape by boat or private plane, the first hotel in San José del Cabo was partly financed by crooner Bing Crosby. Nowadays the town is much more accessible, but its laid-back village charm still prevails.

Jacaranda trees line the boulevards of downtown Plaza Mijares, providing a lilac shade in spring, while a mixture of adobe houses and graceful old mansions hug the streets—a number which have been converted into elegant restaurants and shops. Daytime activities include fishing, kayaking and eco-tours to Sierra de la Laguna, an ecological haven situated between La Paz and Los Cabos, splendid for hiking with its pine forests, oak trees, canyons, hot springs and fossil caves. Several foothill villages provide trails to these forests high up in the mountains, which support a habitat bursting with wildlife and rare plants.

In the last two decades, the Cabos Corridor linking the two cape towns has become a destination in itself, with fishing lodges, wild cliffs, golf courses and exclusive resorts. Recent developments focus on Cabo Real and Cabo del Sol, while its most popular surfing beach, Costa Azul, along with a couple of excellent beaches attracting water-sport fans from around the world. Scuba divers and snorkellers head for the azure Bahía Santa María, a protected marine sanctuary, and Bahía Chileno, an underwater reserve.

Cabo San Lucas is a magnet for the rich and trendy, where cruise ships anchor and beautiful people party all night. This where you will find strips of bars and

nightclubs, along with the dive sites of Roca Pelìcano and Playa Chileno, the natural wonder of Playa del Amor (Lover's Beach), and the sea lion colony of Land's End. Playa del Amor is where the Sea of Cortez meets the Pacific Ocean. Everyday the beach disappears into the turmoil of currents and tumultuous surf, so visitors can arrive in the morning by boat, but will have to leave by evening or they will find themselves trying to swim home. It is a classic spot for romantic sunset sailing by catamaran.

whale-watching

The Californian grey whale (Eschrichtius robustus) can be found in the waters of Baja California Sur. In the 19th century, this species of whale was hunted fiercely and numbers were reduced from 30,000 to about 4,000 between 1858 and 1869. Grey whales were finally taken off the endangered species list in 1992 and their population currently numbers 17,000.

THIS PAGE: *Players can look forward to a scenic golfing experience in Los Cabos.*

OPPOSITE (FROM TOP): *Waterfront dining at Vista Ballenas in Marquis Los Cabos; a swim in the hotel's pool is as inviting as the views of the sea.*

These magnificent creatures spend the summer in solitude in the cold northern waters of the Bering and Chukchi seas, but during autumn, when the sea starts freezing over, they begin their migration south to the warmer waters of Baja California's central Pacific coast. They travel alone or in groups of up to 16 in what is one of the largest mammal migrations in the world. Scientists have observed that despite travelling some 6,000 miles (9,656 km) annually, their arrival at their migration destination is never more than five days late.

The females start their arduous journey across the North-American Pacific ocean, crossing the Gulf of Alaska until they reach the lagoons of Ojo de Liebre, Scammon's Lagoon in Guerrero Negro, San Ignacio and Bahìa Magdalena on the Baja California Peninsula. Here, the saline water allows calves to float and the abundance of prey assists mother whales in producing milk for their hefty young, which can weigh up to 1,102 lb (500 kg) and measure up to 13 ft (4 m) in length. The best time to see them and their newborn calves is from late December to January until March. Births take place in January and February after a gestation period of over a year.

The shallow Laguna Ojo de Liebre (Hare's Eye Lagoon) is a favourite location for sightings in the El Vizcaíno Biosphere Reserve, but the whales can also be found in the lagoons along the Pacific, while humpback and blue whales breed in the Bahía de los Angeles (Bay of Angels).

Bahía Magdalena is the centre for grey whale observation. The surreal landscape of the ever-changing sand dunes provides a dramatic background for Baja's most celebrated visitors. But if you prefer to remain on shore, Cabo San Lucas at the Peninsula's southern tip is a good place to observe the passing whales with your feet planted firmly on the ground.

jumping bean capital

The huge Sonoran Desert, sprouting organ pipe and mammoth saguaro cacti, covers a large northern swathe of the state. Further south, around the capital of Hermosillo, the fertile land is irrigated by rivers and devoted to cattle ranching, agricultural farming and wheat, cotton and citrus production.

Sonora, with its wide expanse of land, is Mexico's second largest state after Chihuahua, and its second most wealthy. Besides manufacturing, agriculture, livestock farming, fishing and aquaculture, the state also has a thriving mining industry.

Puerto Peñasco (Rocky Point) on the northeast coast of the Sea of Cortez, is a popular haunt that attracts legions of weekenders. This small town is known for shrimping and fishing, and has a growing selection of hotels and restaurants. It is close to a nature reserve called the Reserva de la Biósfera El Pinacate y Gran Desierto de Altar, which contains several extinct volcanoes, a cinder mine and vast sand dunes.

Hermosillo is a four-hour drive, 150 miles (241 km) south from the border crossing of Nogales. It was constructed in 1700 by Juan Bautista Escalante for the resettlement of the indigenous Pima Indians. To learn more about the plants and animals of the Sonoran Desert, head for Centro Ecológico de Sonora, the city's zoo and botanical

gardens. Try not to miss the Sonora state fair, a huge cattle show held here from the end of April into the first week of May. San Carlos to the northwest is a popular attraction with tourists because of its combination of shimmering sea and stark desert landscape. The twin-peaked Cerro Tetakawi is the town's most prominent landmark.

The most intriguing city however, must be Álamos. This stretch of the Mexican northwest stirs up images of the Wild West, but Álamos in particular, tucked in the foothills of the Sierra Madre Occidental, has to be Sonora's most authentically restored town. The peaceful village, with its timeless atmosphere, has been declared a national historic monument. It came into wealth in the 17th-century silver mining boom, but was almost destroyed during the run-up to the Mexican Revolution in 1910. Since the 1950s, it has been revived with old haciendas and colonial mansions being carefully restored.

Álamos' buildings have an interesting Moorish influence, skilfully crafted by the 17th-century architects from Andalucía in southern Spain, who filled the winding, cobblestone streets with rustic courtyards laced with beautiful bougainvillea and grand mansions with elaborate façades. Silver was once so abundant it was used as shiny stepping stones of pure silver to guide one rich landowner's daughter from his mansion to the church for her wedding.

Besides history buffs, Álamos is also a draw for nature lovers, being located on the border of two large ecosystems—the desert and tropical jungles of Sinaloa to the south. Over 450 species of birds and animals reside here. Temperatures are welcoming from the end of October to mid-April, but the summer heat can reach a high of 120°F (49°C) between July and August.

If you're in Álamos during the scorching months, be sure to bring home a bag of brincadores (Mexican jumping beans) as Álamos is the 'jumping bean capital' of the world. You can find brincadores in the hills or buy them from the vendors in town. These are actually seed pods, not beans, and they jump because the moth larva inside is trying to spin a web in the pod. The seed pods start to jump when it begins to rain in June and will keep jumping for three to six months until the larva eventually emerges as a moth. You'll find that the hotter the weather, the more these beans jump!

THIS PAGE: A panguero pushing out his boat for whale-watching.

OPPOSITE: Baja's coastal islands provide critical breeding and nesting grounds for seabirds.

The peaceful village, with its timeless atmosphere, has been declared a national historic monument.

Casa Natalia

It used to be the case that tourists doing the Los Cabos route would head straight down to Cabo San Lucas, choosing the bright lights and late-night revelry of the party beach town over the serene charm of San José del Cabo. In recent years, however, the little Spanish colonial town has been drawing visitors of its own who come to enjoy its laid-back ambience, quaint town squares, fine restaurants, and beautifully preserved 18th-century buildings.

And now there's another reason why visitors continue to seek out this charming little village: Casa Natalia, a 16-suite luxury boutique hotel in the heart of town, surrounded by an oasis of magnificent palm trees. A completely renovated historic home, it cleverly combines contemporary Mexican architecture with traditional materials to create an inviting atmosphere. Walls are hand-plastered in vivid blue, yellow and terra cotta and the entire property is a beautiful amalgam of waterfalls and palm trees.

European owners Nathalie and Loïc Tenoux, who live on the premises, have clearly interpreted 'casa' as 'home' and aim to provide a cosy abode at Casa Natalia. Each room is individually decorated and named after its theme such as Conchas (Seashells), Azul (Blue) or Cactus spa suite.

With every detail considered to create a most comfortable and discreetly luxurious environment, rooms are lofty yet cosy with high ceilings, king-sized beds, handcrafted wooden furniture, and Mexican onyx lighting sconces which cast a gentle glow. All rooms have sliding glass doors that open onto private terraces or balconies with hammocks and chairs shaded by flowering bougainvillea and bamboo. Here,

THIS PAGE (CLOCKWISE FROM ABOVE):
Guests can sunbathe beneath an oasis of palm trees; the hotel's contemporary Mexican architecture features handcrafted woodwork; rooms are painted in vivid hues and decorated with Mexican motifs.
OPPOSITE: The heated pool, set against a backdrop of open-flame braziers.

a complimentary breakfast is served to guests relishing the fresh morning breeze. Each of the two spa suites features a private terrace with a large jacuzzi and hammock.

This member of the prestigious Small Luxury Hotels of the World has even built up a reputation for excellent cuisine at Mi Cocina, its sleek and stunning restaurant. Inspired by chef-owner Loïc Tenoux, Mi Cocina tempts with a menu of innovative Mexican-European cuisine that conveys both style and substance.

With a starkly cosmopolitan look to fit the hotel's contemporary Mexican architecture, Mi Cocina's design is as refreshing as its food. Guests dine on lava-stone and linen-covered limestone tables, while classic Villeroy and Boch china is juxtaposed with modern silver and glassware. Floor-to-ceiling glass doors offer a glimpse of the cascading waterfall in the lush courtyard filled with palm trees and flaming braziers.

After dinner, guests can enjoy margaritas and Martinis in the outdoor Palapa Bar or take a walk to the picturesque town square with its cobblestone streets and fountains. A stone's throw from the town's focal point, the twin towers of Iglesia San José, and the exotic San José del Cabo estuary and preserve, Casa Natalia is ideally situated for visitors to experience the culture, cuisine, beaches, golf courses and nature the place has to offer.

PHOTOGRAPHS COURTESY OF CASA NATALIA.

FACTS

ROOMS	14 deluxe double rooms • 2 spa suites
FOOD	Mi Cocina Restaurant: innovative Mexican-European
DRINK	Palapa Bar
FEATURES	contemporary Mexican architecture • heated pool • waterfalls • in-room spa services • free shuttle to the beach • whale-watching tours, kayaking and hiking on request
NEARBY	shops, cafés and restaurants of San José del Cabo • San José del Cabo estuary • historic artist colony of Todos Santos
CONTACT	Boulevard Mijares 4, San José del Cabo, Baja California Sur 23400 • telephone: +52.624 142 5100 • facsimile: +52.624 142 5110 • email: questions@casanatalia.com • website: www.casanatalia.com

Hotel California

The small, laid-back town of Todos Santos has been regarded as on oasis on the desert highway between Cabo San Lucas and La Paz. And when visitors come across Hotel California, the focal point of the town, they're likely to think they're seeing a mirage. Warm and vibrant with its sunrise-hued walls and tree-lined streets, it's hard to miss Hotel California amid the sleepy streets of Todos Santos. In fact, the 100-year-old building has pretty much become a landmark of the place, even a legend for those who believe it was the inspiration for the famous Eagles' song.

Tourists traipsing round the old town are inevitably drawn to the hotel with its impressive and airy lobby. In keeping with the energetic, surfer feel of the original hostel, the ambience is deliberately casual and lively. Red Spanish tiles cover the floors, turqoise blue walls are a reminder of the nearby ocean, and sofas, cushions and ethnic carpets are a riot of bright Mexican colours.

Rooms are luxurious, comfortable and generously large after its original 20 rooms were knocked down to create 11 exclusive rooms. All are washed in cheerful citrus shades and have balconies with great views.

...the 100-year-old building has pretty much become a landmark of the place...

THIS PAGE *(CLOCKWISE FROM LEFT):*
*The courtyard and pool,
with many shady niches
for guests to relax in;
a chandelier of hand-blown
coloured glass hangs in the lobby.*

OPPOSITE *(FROM TOP): Meals can be
had in the courtyard by the
fountains and gazebo;
formerly a surfer's lodge, Hotel
California is now an upbeat
and upscale retreat with
modern amenities.*

The revamped Hotel California is the work of its Canadian owners who were drawn to Todos Santos for its natural tranquillity and artistic vibe. Devoted to showing the best of the town, the hotel makes itself a showcase for the art of local artists. The premise is in itself a work of art and has become a popular venue for fashion shoots, and the subject of much international publicity. Undoubtedly, Hotel California has become *the* place to stay in, and soon, more luxuries such as a spa can be expected.

Certainly no surfer food hut, the elegant La Coronela is always serves seafood that is freshly caught locally, bread baked on the same day, and desserts made on its premises. The menu is also light-hearted enough to offer burgers and gourmet sandwiches which diners might want to enjoy with fine wine.

That is perhaps what is infinitely appealing about Hotel California—private and luxurious, yet very much in keeping with the spirit of its past...and, if you believe, the lyrics of the legendary *Hotel California.*

FACTS		
	ROOMS	11 rooms and suites
	FOOD	La Coronela Restaurante: Mexican-Mediterranean fusion
	DRINK	Hotel California Bar
	FEATURES	pool • library • meditation room • shop selling Mexican and international art
	BUSINESS	travel agency • secretarial services at reception desk
	NEARBY	Todos Santos town • Cabo San Lucas • La Paz
	CONTACT	Calle Benito Juarez e/ Morelos y Marquez de Leon, A.P. 48, Todos Santos, Baja California Sur 23305 • telephone: +52.612 145 0525 • facsimile: +52.612 145 0288 • email: hotelcaliforniareservations@hotmail.com

PHOTOGRAPHS COURTESY OF HOTEL CALIFORNIA.

Las Ventanas al Paraíso

Los Cabos claims to see more private planes land here than any other resort destination in the world, including Palm Beach, Florida. The rich and famous began flocking to this area more than half a century ago, when superstars of the day such as John Wayne and Bing Crosby flew down for the world-class marlin fishing.

The glitterati continue to converge at Los Cabos. This resort city at the southern tip of the Baja Peninsula has irresistible allure—glorious year-round sunshine and rugged landscape melding mountains, deserts and sea—not to mention the unsurpassed fishing and other activities from horseback riding to sailing. But these days, the Hollywood crowd and celebrities from the sports and business worlds visit Los Cabos in increasing numbers for an altogether different reason: Las Ventanas al Paraíso.

The 61-suite resort is the ultimate oasis, where even celebrities used to the highest standards of service and pampering are made to feel extra special. Since its opening in 1997, Las Ventanas' efforts have been recognised in the countless awards it has received for excellent service and hospitality.

Managed by the acclaimed Rosewood Hotels and Resorts, Las Ventanas is a cocoon-like village linked together by mosaic paths inlaid with thousands of smooth pebbles. These pebble motifs accentuate the entire resort—from the guestrooms to the public areas—and are one of many elements designed to complement the property's natural surroundings. Small buildings merge Mexican and Mediterranean architecture with the colour of sand. Exotic desert plants and cacti fill the gardens and courtyards, keeping the Sonoran desert ever present. And the

serpentine network of infinity swimming pools appears to float on the horizon, melding seamlessly into the azure waters of the Sea of Cortez.

Even when every suite is occupied, Las Ventanas is remarkably quiet, and each guest feels ensconced in a secluded, private world. You can wander around the grounds believing you're the only one fortunate enough to have discovered this gem, when actually, suites are so lavish and comfortable that guests never want to leave them. Exceptionally spacious, starting at 960 sq ft (89 sq m), they are exquisitely decorated with hand-carved appointments such as cedar doors, inlaid-pebble headboards, seashell-tiled floors and opaque mother-of-pearl windows. The centrepiece of the suites are the beds—perhaps the most indulgent anywhere—nestled on raised palatial platforms with the finest cotton sheets, goose-down duvets and plush pillows.

From your bed, the suite opens up to spectacular panoramas of the deep-blue sea and colourful gardens. You can soak in the private jacuzzi on your patio, or dive into your very own infinity pool in any of the one-bedroom suites. On a cool winter evening, enjoy a roaring fire in the fireplace. You can use your personal telescope to gaze at the

heavens or spot dolphins or grey whales that journey from the cold north to the warm Baja waters for the winter.

If you do decide to venture out from your suite, however, delightful options await. Las Ventanas boasts one of the world's most elite spas. Choose from a sumptuous menu of massages, facials, body treatments and therapies from around the world. The spa experience can also be enjoyed on the private Beach Pavilion, or at sea onboard the hotel's plush yacht.

As impeccable as the resort's facilities are, it is the polished service and attention to detail that have made Las Ventanas an international star. At the poolside, every whim and need of the guests is attended to by the pool butlers. They offer personal CD players and CDs, books and magazines, cold towels and chilled mineral water, as well as food and drinks from the Sea Grill.

If you are lounging on the beach under a thatched palapa, attendants will also see to your needs and even provide a unique wake-up service. Raise a flag at your hammock to indicate the time that you want the attendant to come by, and he will gently wake you with the soft sounds of a traditional Mexican bell. At the Tequila and Ceviche Bar, the 'tequilero' will select the perfect tequila for you, whether for sipping or mixing in a margarita, or as a shooter.

And then there are details are so subtle you could easily miss them. The sewing kit placed in your suite for example, has been customised to match the colours of your wardrobe and needles are pre-threaded with the predominant shades. The turndown service is made even more luxurious with in-suite aromatherapy. And at Las Ventanas, every staff member knows your name and suite number.

...each guest feels ensconced in a secluded, private world.

Las Ventanas is warm and sleepy during the day, but comes alive at night. Lanterns with burning candles line the paths and flicker throughout the grounds, while guests savour cocktails and live music in the lounge, gourmet cuisine in The Restaurant, and contemporary Mexican cooking at the Sea Grill on the water's edge.

Or you can opt for a romantic evening for two in your room with a beautifully arranged, candle-lit table on your patio, or on the rooftop terrace, where you can gaze at the brilliant display of stars overhead. After all, Las Ventanas al Paraíso does mean 'windows to paradise'.

FACTS

ROOMS	61 suites with choice of garden view, ocean view or on the ocean front.
FOOD	The Restaurant: Baja-Mediterranean • Sea Grill: casual dining at the water's edge
DRINK	Tequila and Ceviche Bar: aged tequila and fresh ceviche • La Cava: wine
FEATURES	fitness centre • spa • 4 pools • 2 tennis courts • video library
BUSINESS	conference centre • Internet access • ocean-view patio for meetings and events
NEARBY	6 golf courses • Sea of Cortez • Cabo San Lucas • San José del Cabo • San José del Cabo international airport
CONTACT	Carretera Transpeninsular km 19.5, San José del Cabo, Baja California Sur 23400 • telephone: +52.624 144 0300 • facsimile: +52.624 114 0301 • email: lasventanas@rosewoodhotels.com • website: www.lasventanas.com

Marquis Los Cabos

Visitors to the Los Cabos area in Mexico are divided when it comes to holidays by the sea. Some are attracted to the glamour of its famous luxury hotels, while others prefer to take the rural route to experience its charm and character. Marquis Los Cabos Beach, Golf, Spa and Casitas Resort is the latest destination where you can have it all.

Because of its fortuitous location at the southern tip of Baja California where the tranquil desert meets the untamed ocean, Marquis Los Cabos opens up to a spectacular countryside and coastline where deep-sea fishing tempts with possibilities of sailfish and blue marlin catches, and the dramatic reefs in the Sea of Cortez offer unmatchable diving experiences.

And yet for those who are reluctant to give up their creature comforts for some rugged adventure, Marquis Los Cabos delivers the ultimate in indulgence.

...privacy and romance rule the day at the hotel's 28 exclusive casitas with private pools.

For one, the 237-suite hotel, which opened in 2003, is tucked between two leading 18-hole golf courses, the Cabo Real Course and the renowned Cabo del Sol Ocean Course which occupies the 68th place on *Golf Magazine*'s poll of 'Top 100 Courses in the World'.

The hotel's spa—the largest in Los Cabos—is outfitted with open-air jacuzzis, saunas and steam baths, and features a range of holistic treatments that uses indigenous ingredients such as cactus oils, sea salt and seaweed hauled from the Sea of Cortez. The adjoining fitness centre rewards its visitors with magnificent views of the glistening sea.

Surrounded by lush gardens filled with native plants, palm trees and cacti, privacy and romance rule the day at the hotel's 28 exclusive casitas with private pools. Frette bed linen, Bvlgari toiletries, goose-down comforters, and hydro-massage baths

with ocean views and private balconies are among the other features found at these stylish homes by the beach that put the extra shine on the hotel's fifth star.

A gallery for the dynamic works of Latin America's leading artists, the suites and hallways are designed as a homage to contemporary Mexican architecture and Santa Fe traditions.

Take a stroll through the beautifully landscaped grounds to the alfresco lobby and witness the clever use of the ocean as a backdrop and the sounds of a dramatic 36-ft (11-m) waterfall gushing into the main swimming pool below as background music.

Splendid meals await at the hotel's three restaurants, while breakfast is delivered quietly and unobtrusively through small alcoves to the rooms every morning.

It is the height of luxury here at Marquis Los Cabos, where intimate details co-exist with stunning grandeur.

THIS PAGE (FROM TOP): Modern Mexican architecture with rustic touches; a waterfall drops over the bar into the main pool.

OPPOSITE (FROM TOP): Postcard perspective from the lobby; all casitas come with private pools.

PHOTOGRAPHS COURTESY OF MARQUIS LOS CABOS.

FACTS		
ROOMS	203 junior suites • 28 casitas • 5 Marquis suites • 1 presidential suite	
FOOD	Canto del Mar: gourmet • Vista Ballenas: Californian and Mexican • Dos Mares Restaurant and Bar: seafood • Kosher food on request	
DRINK	El Suspiro: lobby bar	
FEATURES	fitness centre • holistic spa • waterfall • 3 pools • jacuzzis • saunas • steam baths	
BUSINESS	meeting rooms • boardroom • conference centre • Internet access • audio-visual equipment	
NEARBY	2 golf courses • shops at San José del Cabo and Cabo San Lucas	
CONTACT	Carretera Transpeninsular km 21.5, Fraccionamiento Cabo Real, San José del Cabo, Baja California Sur 23400 • telephone: +1.877.238 9399 (US) or +52.624 144 2000 • facsimile: +52.624 144 2001 • email: information@marquisloscabos.com • website: www.marquisloscabos.com	

The Westin Regina Golf + Beach Resort Los Cabos

What a dramatic way to end miles of desert—in sweeping vermillion architecture flanked by lofty mountains and a brilliantly white beach. Considered an architectural triumph, the nine-storey building of The Westin Regina Golf and Beach Resort has become an important landmark of the Los Cabos area. It imaginatively mirrors the desert mountains with red native stone cladding, and pays tribute to the sea with its sensual curved structure. At the lobby, one can view the curve of the hotel forming a bridge to seamlessly join the two cliffs on either side of the sprawling grounds.

Situated at the tip of the Baja Peninsula, the 243-room hotel enjoys its own pristine strip of beach, while the sea offers a vista of azure as far as the eye can see. Boasting a dramatic location at Land's End, where the Sea of Cortez meets the Pacific Ocean, the hotel makes the most of its stunning surroundings with unbeatable views from every room. Within its grounds, guests are greeted with a striking palette of Mexican colours—bright accents of fuschia, amber and green are contrasted against the red of the surrounding desert.

While the design of The Westin Regina is undoubtedly state-of-the-art, its facilities are

THIS PAGE (CLOCKWISE FROM TOP):
Curvaceous blue pools add to the visual feast of this oasis; the magnitude of the resort's architecture is best appreciated from the lobby; interiors are luxurious yet cosy.
OPPOSITE: Created by Mexican architect, Javier Sordo Medaleno, the cutting-edge design is a modern interpretation of the ultimate beach resort.

...fuschia, amber and green are contrasted against the red of the surrounding desert.

similarly impressive. Its recreational activities are so plentiful, it's possible to stay here for a week and still find something new to do everyday. Guests usually head first for one of seven golf courses nearby. Then, it's a choice of seven swimming pools, volleyball, water sports and tennis.

The spa, however, is its crowning glory with world-class amenities and friendly Mexican service. Besides the treatment rooms, saunas, steam room and whirlpool, it also offers a beauty salon for facials and a variety of relaxing massages. The fitness centre is modern and professionally outfitted with computerised exercise equipment and exercise studios.

Most guests, however, leave at least a day to spend in their plush rooms. All have private balconies to enjoy unforgettable sunsets, and within, guests are indulged with five-star amenities including marble baths, handcrafted furniture and the most luxurious

shower facilities. It would be most tempting to have room service delivered daily, but it would be a shame to miss out on the four restaurants that offer a selection of Mexican-inspired menus. Arrecifes is the sophisticated dining room overlooking the Sea of Cortez, while La Cascada provides entertainment

along with themed dinners. El Set, the grill restaurant, and La Playa, the poolside lunch venue provide casual eats.

With the number of activities and pampering options offered on the premises, guests at The Westin Regina have certainly found their own perfect oasis.

FACTS

ROOMS	190 rooms • 39 Royal Beach Club rooms • 14 suites
FOOD	Arrecifes: Mexican gourmet • La Cascada: Mexican and international • El Set: grilled local specialities • La Playa: poolside dining
DRINK	La Playa bar • La Cantina
FEATURES	fitness centre • spa • 7 pools • 2 tennis courts • 7 golf courses
BUSINESS	meeting facilities • audio-visual equipment
NEARBY	Los Cabos • Cabo San Lucas
CONTACT	Carretera Transpenisular km 22.5, San José Del Cabo, Baja California Sur 23400 • telephone: +52.624 145 8000 • facsimile: +52.624 145 8008/6152 • email: reservations.01087@westin.com • website: www.westinloscabos.com

PHOTOGRAPHS COURTESY OF THE WESTIN REGINA GOLF AND BEACH RESORT LOS CABOS.

Hacienda de Los Santos

For the last 50 years, Mexico has been a powerful magnet for those dreaming of escape. But if lounging on hammocks overlooking the sea isn't your idea of an ideal getaway, Mexico offers another kind of attraction altogether. For some, the culture and rich history of the country are as appealing as its seaside scene. If walking along cobblestone streets, admiring the vestiges of the conquistador past, and singing along to Spanish troubadours is what you're looking for, come to Álamos, Mexico's best-kept secret.

Located in the foothills of Sierra Madre in Sonora, Álamos is among the country's most splendid colonial cities. Its inhabitants have included conquistadors, mining barons, imperialists and revolutionaries. Step into any of the town squares and you'll enter a different age of Spanish romanticism and old Mexico.

In keeping with the elegant richness of its surroundings is Hacienda de Los Santos, the former residence of a wealthy silver baron, now converted into a 23-room hotel in the heart of the colonial city. Built in the 17th century, the property has been restored and expanded by the Swickard family, who live on the premises and manage the hacienda. Much of the original structure has been retained—guests get to luxuriate

THIS PAGE (CLOCKWISE FROM ABOVE):
The 17th-century hacienda is surrounded by natural landscape; entertainment is provided at the hotel's theatre.

OPPOSITE (CLOCKWISE FROM LEFT):
Rooms are adorned with Spanish colonial furnishings and rustic fireplaces; a grand piano takes centrestage in the majestic theatre; warm nights are best spent soaking in the outdoor pool.

If it's an escape you're looking for, Hacienda de Los Santos is as good as it gets.

by fireplaces in spacious rooms, enjoy flower-filled courtyards with sweeping arches, and have their meals in grand colonial dining rooms.

The warm hospitality of the owners makes the hacienda much more attractive. They occasionally join guests at dinner, which is an elegant candlelit affair with silver and crystal tableware, and Mexican cuisine using organic produce from the hotel's own ranch. After dinner, guests can relax in one of the many alcoves while being serenaded by the resident quartet, Los Hacendados. They could also watch movies in the theatre or browse through the extensive library. They could even sit in on an introductory course to Mexico's most famous drink at the 125-year-old Zapata's Cantina, which offers over 400 different tequilas.

The next day can be spent exploring the vast ecological treasures of Álamos and its unique tropical forest, a natural habitat for vast species of birds that stretches all the way to Costa Rica. Alternatively, the quaint Álamos square is only a five-minute walk away.

Back at the hacienda, there are more relaxing pursuits in store: savouring artworks at the newly opened Hacienda Gallery, enjoying a massage at the new full-service spa, sunbathing by any of the four mosaic-tiled pools, or simply strolling through the expansive grounds. If it's an escape you're looking for, Hacienda de Los Santos is as good as it gets.

FACTS

ROOMS	23 rooms
FOOD	San Juan, San Felipe, San Ángel and Santa Ana dining rooms: contemporary Mexican with Euro-American influence
DRINK	Zapata's Cantina
FEATURES	4 pools • spa • fitness centre • theatre • Hacienda Gallery • 2 putting greens
BUSINESS	conference room
NEARBY	museum • cathedral • beaches • Álamos • Mayan villages
CONTACT	Calle Molina 8, Álamos, Sonora 85763 • telephone: +52.647 428 0222 • facsimile: +52.647 428 0367 • email: info@haciendadelossantos.com • website: www.haciendadelossantos.com

PHOTOGRAPHS COURTESY OF HACIENDA DE LOS SANTOS.

Aeromexico

What's the fastest way to paradise? On Aeromexico, it seems. With its world record for being number one in punctuality, you'll be on the sunny shores of Playa del Carmen with a daiquiri in hand before you can say 'La Bamba.' In fact, the airline runs advertisements in South America saying that if you're running a few minutes late, don't bother rushing, the plane's already taken off.

With such an extraordinary record, it's no wonder Aeromexico has received numerous accolades from aviation institutions around the world highlighting its world-class standards. Within the Latin American skies, the airline has achieved many firsts, like being the first to develop an electronic ticketing system and a business class standard, as well as a frequent flier programme, Club Premiere.

Ultimately, it's the experience on an Aeromexico flight which makes the difference. Step on board and it seems your holiday's already started. The airline scores on the finer points of service which differentiate it from the rest. It may be something as inconsequential as a piece of candy for passengers as they are welcomed on board, free drinks and pretzels at some connecting airports, or a free margarita on the flight. But such small gestures go a long way in enhancing the overall pleasure of flying with Aeromexico. The highlight, however, must be the seamlessly efficient and friendly service. Phone calls to reservation centres are answered promptly, check-in counters move quickly, and on-board hospitality goes beyond the expected with friendly Spanish- and English-speaking staff who strive to fulfil every request.

Then there are the more glamorous features of the airline, such as the 'Suns and Spices' programme for Clase Premier (business class) passengers, designed to promote gourmet Mexican cuisine to all parts of the world. Featuring traditional Mexican recipes, the menu on international flights is created by French chef Thierry Blouet, while the one on national flights is planned by the chefs of Presidente Intercontinental Hotel. Both offer pleasant surprises for many passengers who marvel at the colourful taste spectrum of Mexican gastronomy.

Equal emphasis is given to the choice of wines. Set up by famed Mexican sommelier Pedro Poncelis Brambila, the airline's vast wine cellar in the sky, which includes selections from Mexican winery Monte Xanic, has gained much recognition and awards for Aeromexico.

In between meals, passengers are given such a wide choice of entertainment options, time literally flies. More than 10 movies and nine music channels are available. But of course, the best way to begin one's holiday is a peaceful slumber. In Clase Premier, it's hard to get a better rest than on its spacious, plush seats that offer a 140-degree inclination—all dressed in covers and pillows when you're ready for your undisturbed snooze. And before you know it, you would have arrived at your destination, departing from Mexico's friendly skies to its gorgeous beaches and beaming weather.

THIS PAGE AND OPPOSITE: The fine cuisine served on board Aeromexico's flights is in itself the most alluring invitation to visit the country.

FACTS

FOOD	traditional Mexican
DRINK	winelist composed by Mexican sommelier Pedro Poncelis Brambila
FEATURES	Club Premier frequent flier programme • in-flight entertainment features over 10 movie and 9 music channels in 4 languages • portable DVD player on request • over 29 newspapers, 22 magazines and L'Occitane amenities for Clase Premier passengers
BUSINESS	Internet access
CONTACT	telephone: +1.800.237 6639 (US), +1.800.247 3737 (Club Premier, US), +34.91.548 9810 (Spain), +56.2.390 1000 (Chile), +55.11.3253 3888 (Brazil), +51.1.421 3500 (Peru) or +33.1.5504 9010 (France) • website: www.premier@aeromexico.com.mx

PHOTOGRAPHS COURTESY OF AEROMEXICO.

index

index

picturecredits

directory

Aeromexico
telephone : +1.800.237 6639 (US)
+1.800.247 3737 (Club Premier, US)
+34.91.548 9810 (Spain)
+56.2.390 1000 (Chile)
+55.11.3253 3888 (Brazil)
+51.1.421 3500 (Peru)
+33.1.5504 9010 (France)
www.premier@aeromexico.com.mx

Casa Cid de León
Avenida Morelos 602, Centro Histórico, Oaxaca 68000
telephone : +52.951 514 1893
facsimile : +52.951 514 7013
reservaciones@casaciddeleon.com
www.casaciddeleon.com

Casa Natalia
Boulevard Mijares 4, San José del Cabo,
Baja California Sur 23400
telephone : +52.624 142 5100
facsimile : +52.624 142 5110
questions@casanatalia.com
www.casanatalia.com

Casa Tamayo Cuernavaca
Rufino Tamayo 26, Colonia Acapatzingo, Cuernavaca,
Morelos 62440
telephone : +52.777 318 9477
facsimile : +52.777 312 8186
lasmusas@casatamayo.com.mx
www.casatamayo.com

Camino Real Oaxaca
Calle 5 de Mayo 300, Oaxaca 68000
telephone : +52.951 501 6100
facsimile : +52.951 516 0732
oax@caminoreal.com
www.caminoreal.com/oaxaca

Camino Real Zaashila Huatulco
Boulevard Benito Juárez 5, Bahía de Tangolunda,
Bahía de Huatulco, Oaxaca 70989
telephone : +52.958 581 0460
facsimile : +52.958 581 0461
zaa@caminoreal.com
www.caminoreal.com/zaashila

Ceiba del Mar Spa Resort
Costera Norte, Lote 1, Smz 10, Puerto Morelos,
Quintana Roo 77580
telephone : +52.998 872 8060
facsimile : +52.998 872 8061
reserve@ceibadelmar.com
www.ceibadelmar.com

Deseo [Hotel + Lounge]
5a Avenue Y Calle 12, Playa del Carmen,
Quintana Roo 77710
telephone : +52.984 879 3620
facsimile : +52.984 879 3621
info@hoteldeseo.com
www.hoteldeseo.com

El Careyes Beach Resort
Carretera km 53.5, Barra de Navidad, Costa Careyes,
Jalisco 48983
telephone : +52.315 351 0000
facsimile : +52.315 351 0100
careyes@grupoplan.com
www.starwood.com/careyes

El Sueño Hotel + Spa
9 Oriente 12, Centro Histórico, Puebla City, Puebla 72000
telephone : +52.222 232 6489
facsimile : +52.222 232 6423
hfdzdelara@elsueno-hotel.com
www.elsueno-hotel.com

El Tamarindo Golf Resort
Carretera Melaque y Puerto Vallarta km 7.5, Cihuatlán,
Jalisco 48970
telephone : +52.315 351 5032
facsimile : +52.315 351 5070
tamarindo@grupoplan.com
www.luxurycollection.com

Four Seasons Resort Punta Mita
Punta Mita, Bahía de Banderas, Nayarit 63734
telephone : +52.329 191 6000
facsimile : +52.329 291 6060
res.puntamita@fourseasons.com
www.fourseasons.com

HABITA
Avenida Presidente Masaryk 201, Colonia Polanco,
Mexico City 11560
telephone : +52.555 282 3100
facsimile : +52.555 282 3101
info@hotelhabita.com
www.hotelhabita.com

Hacienda de Los Santos
Calle Molina 8, Alamos, Sonora 85763
telephone : +52.647 428 0222
facsimile : +52.647 428 0367
info@haciendadelossantos.com
www.haciendadelossantos.com

Hacienda los Laureles
Hidalgo 21, San Felipe del Agua,
Oaxaca 68020
telephone : +52.951 501 5300
facsimile : +52.951 501 5301
bookings@hotelhaciendalaslaureles.com
inquiry@hotelhaciendalaslaureles.com
www.hotelhaciendalaslaureles.com
www.hotelhaciendalaslaureles-spa.com

Hacienda San José
Carretera Tixkokob-Tekanto km 30, Tixkokob,
Yucatán 97470
telephone : +52.999 910 4617
facsimile : +52.999 923 7963
reservations1@grupoplan.com
www.starwood.com

Hacienda Santa Rosa
Carretera Mérida km 129, Campeche, Santa Rosa,
Yucatán 97800
telephone : +52.999 910 4852
facsimile : +52.999 923 7963
reservations1@grupoplan.com
www.starwood.com

Hacienda Temozón
Carretera Mérida-Uxmal km 182,
Temozón Sur Yucatán 97825
telephone : +52.999 923 8089
facsimile : +52.999 923 7963
temozon@grupoplan.com
www.starwood.com

Hacienda Uayamón
Carretera China-Edzná km 20, Uayamón, Campeche
telephone : +52.981 829 7526
facsimile : +52.999 923 7963
reservations1@grupoplan.com
www.starwood.com

Hacienda Xcanatún
Mérida-Progreso Highway km 12, Xcanatún Mérida,
Yucatán 97300
telephone : +52.999 941 0213
facsimile : +52.999 941 0319
hacienda@xcanatun.com
www.xcanatun.com

Hotel California
Calle Benito Juarez e/ Morelos y Marquez de Leon,
A.P. 48, Todos Santos, Baja California Sur 23305
telephone : +52.612 145 0525
facsimile : +52.612 145 0288
hotelcaliforniareservations@hotmail.com

Hotelito Desconocido
Playon de Mismaloya, Natural Reserve,
60 miles (96 km) south of Puerto Vallarta
telephone : +52.322 222 2526
facsimile : +52.322 223 0293
hotelito@hotelito.com
www.hotelito.com

Hotel Los Juaninos
Morelos Sur 39, Centro Histórico, Morelia, Michoacán 58000
telephone : +52.443 312 0036
facsimile : +52.443 312 0036
reservaciones@hoteljuaninos.com.mx
www.hoteljuaninos.com.mx

Ikal del Mar
Playa Xcalacoco, Riviera Maya, Quintana Roo 77710
telephone : +52.713 528 7863
facsimile : +52.713 528 3697
reservations@ikaldelmar.com
www.ikaldelmar.com

La Quinta Luna
3 Sur 702, Cholula, Puebla 72760
telephone : +52.222 247 8915
facsimile : +52.222 247 8916
reservaciones@laquintaluna.com
www.laquintaluna.com

Las Brisas Acapulco
Carretera Escénica 5255, Fraccionamiento Las Brisas,
Acapulco, Guerrero 39867
telephone : +52.744 469 6900
facsimile : +52.744 446 5328
brisa@brisas.com.mx
www.brisas.com.mx

Las Ventanas al Paraíso
Carretera Transpeninsular km 19.5, San José del Cabo,
Baja California Sur 23400
telephone : +52.624 144 0300
facsimile : +52.624 144 0301
lasventanas@rosewoodhotels.com
www.lasventanas.com

Mahakua—Hacienda de San Antonio
Municipio de Comala, Colima 28450
telephone : +52.312 313 4411
facsimile : +52.312 314 3727
hacienda@mahakua.com.mx
reservations@amanresorts.com
www.amanresorts.com

Maroma Resort + Spa
Highway 307, Riviera Maya km 51, Quintana Roo 77710
telephone : +52.998 872 8200
facsimile : +52.998 872 8220
reservations@maromahotel.com
www.maromahotel.com

Marquis Los Cabos
Carretera Transpeninsular km 21.5, Fraccionamiento Cabo
Real, San José del Cabo, Baja California Sur 23400
telephone : +1.877.238 9399 (US)
+52.624 144 2000
facsimile : +52.624 144 2001
information@marquisloscabos.com
www.marquisloscabos.com

Mesón Sacristía de Capuchinas
9 Oriente 16, Antigua Calle de Capuchinas,
Centro Histórico, Puebla 72000
telephone : +1.800.712 4028
+52.222 246 6084
facsimile : +52.222 232 8088
sacristia@mesones-sacristia.com
www.mesones-sacristia.com

Mesón Sacristía de la Compañía
6 Sur 304, Callejón de los Sapos, Centro Histórico,
Puebla 72000
telephone : +1.800.712 4028
+52.222 232 3554
facsimile : +52.222 232 4513
sacristia@mesones-sacristia.com
www.mesones-sacristia.com

Mosquito Blue
Quinta Avenida Entre 12 to 14, Playa del Carmen,
Quintana Roo 77710
telephone : +52.984 873 1335
facsimile : +52.984 873 1337
information@mosquitoblue.com
www.mosquitoblue.com

Na Balam
Calle Zazil Ha 118, Playa Norte, Isla Mujeres,
Quintana Roo 77400
telephone : +52.998 877 0279
facsimile : +52.998 877 0446
nabalam@nabalam.com
www.nabalam.com

Paraíso de la Bonita Resort + Thalasso
Bahía Petenpich km 328, Cancún,
Quintana Roo 7750
telephone : +52.998 872 8300
facsimile : +52.998 872 8301
resa@paraisodelabonitaresort.com
www.paraiso-bonita.intercontinental.com

Posada la Basílica
6 Arciga, Pátzcuaro, Michoacán 61600
telephone : +1.800.288 4282 (US)
+52.434 342 1108
facsimile : +52.434 342 0659
hotelpb@hotmail.com
www.posadalabasilica.com

Quinta las Acacias
Paseo de la Presa 168, Guanajuato 36000
telephone : +52.473 731 1517
facsimile : +52.473 731 1862
acacias@int.com.mx
www.quintalasacacias.com.mx
www.mexicoboutiquehotels.com/lasacacias

Secreto
Sección Rocas, Lote 11, Punta Norte, Isla Mujeres,
Quintana Roo 77400
telephone : +52.998 877 1039
facsimile : +52.998 877 1048
reserv@hotelsecreto.com
www.hotelsecreto.com

Shangri-La Caribe
Calle 38 Norte con Zona Federal Marítima,
Playa del Carmen, Quintana Roo 77710
telephone : +52.984 873 0591
facsimile : +52.984 873 0500
info@shangrilacaribe.net
www.shangrilacaribe.net

The Westin Regina Golf + Beach Resort Los Cabos
Carretera Transpeninsular km 22.5, San José Del Cabo,
Baja California Sur 23400
telephone : +52.624 145 8000
facsimile : +52.624 145 8008/6152
reservations.01087@westin.com
www.westinloscabos.com

Verana
Yelapa, Puerto Vallarta, Jalisco 48319
telephone : +1.800.677 5156 (US)
+52.322 209 5107
ana@verana.com
www.verana.com

Villa del Sol
Playa la Ropa s/n, Zihuatanejo, Guerrero 40880
telephone : +52.755 555 5500
facsimile : +52.755 554 2758
reservation@hotelvilladelsol.net
www.hotelvilladelsol.net

Villa Montaña
Patzimba 201, Colonia Vista Bella, Morelia,
Michoacán 58090
telephone : +52.443 314 0231
facsimile : +52.443 315 1423
reservaciones@villamontana.com.mx
www.villamontana.com.mx

W Mexico City
Campos Eliseos 252, Colonia Polanco,
Mexico City 11560
telephone : +52.559 138 1800
facsimile : +52.555 208 4090
reservations.mexicocity@whotels.com
www.whotels.com